The Teaching Improvement Agenda

T0383775

Drawing on ten years of research into whole-of-school teaching improvement, this engaging text explains what teaching improvement requires, how it is achieved, and how to maintain it in your classroom and school.

Based on studies involving real schools and real teachers, *The Teaching Improvement Agenda* is focused on what really matters for teachers and leaders in today's schools. The book begins with an examination of the education field to identify the fundamental elements which inform and generate teaching improvement. This lays the foundations for an instructive set of innovative, research-informed strategies which have been designed to empower the teacher and school leader to improve teaching across the whole school. The book closes with a series of case studies that demonstrate these approaches in action.

Answering the "what?" and "how?" questions of teaching improvement, this book is an essential guide for school leaders and teachers, as well as instructors and students in initial teacher education.

David Lynch, Professor of Education and Research Leader of TeachLab, Southern Cross University, Australia.

Richard Smith, Adjunct Professor, Southern Cross University and Emeritus Professor, Central Queensland University, Australia.

David Turner, Deputy Research Leader, TeachLab, Southern Cross University, Australia.

Barnett Berry, Senior Research Fellow, Learning Policy Institute, South Carolina, United States.

Jake Madden, Group Head of Schools, Aoba Schools Group, Japan.

David Spendlove, Associate Dean, Faculty of Humanities, Manchester University, UK.

Megan Lee, Senior Teaching Fellow, Bond University, Australia.

The Teaching Improvement Agenda

What Matters and How Teaching Excellence Is Achieved

David Lynch, Richard Smith,
David Turner, Barnett Berry,
Jake Madden, David Spendlove,
and Megan Lee

Routledge
Taylor & Francis Group

LONDON AND NEW YORK

Designed cover image: © Jose Luis Pelaez Inc/Getty Images

First published 2025
by Routledge
4 Park Square, Milton Park, Abingdon, Oxon OX14 4RN

and by Routledge
605 Third Avenue, New York, NY 10158

Routledge is an imprint of the Taylor & Francis Group, an informa business

British Library Cataloguing-in-Publication Data
A catalogue record for this book is available from the British Library

Library of Congress Cataloging-in-Publication Data
Names: Lynch, David (Professor of Education), author.
Title: The teaching improvement agenda : what matters and how teaching excellence is achieved / David Lynch, Richard Smith, David Spendlove, Barnett Berry, Jake Madden, David Turner and Megan Lee
Description: Abingdon, Oxon ; New York, NY : Routledge, 2025. | Includes bibliographical references and index.
Identifiers: LCCN 2024014860 | ISBN 9781032300689 (hardback) | ISBN 9781032300672 (paperback) | ISBN 9781003303312 (ebook)
Subjects: LCSH: Teaching–Methodology. | Teachers–In-service training.
Classification: LCC LB1025.3 .L96 2025 |
DDC 371.102–dc23/eng/20240429
LC record available at https://lccn.loc.gov/2024014860

ISBN: 978-1-032-30068-9 (hbk)
ISBN: 978-1-032-30067-2 (pbk)
ISBN: 978-1-003-30331-2 (ebk)

DOI: 10.4324/9781003303312

Typeset in Galliard
by Taylor & Francis Books

Contents

Tables

About the authors

David Lynch is a Professor in the Faculty of Education and research director for the research entity TeachLab at Southern Cross University in Australia. He is the author of numerous books and articles on teacher education and teaching improvement, specialising in whole-of-school teaching improvement. He is a pioneer in teacher education, having led major reviews and redevelopments of teacher education in Australia, as well as school transformation projects both in Australia and overseas. His background is in primary education, having been a teacher and senior state school principal in early professional life before joining academia.

Richard Smith has extensive experience in school and higher education teaching, administration, and governance since the 1960s. He has a distinguished record in research, publication, postgraduate supervision, policy development, academic journal creation and editorship, as well as in professional associations. His career-long interests include the conceptualisation and development of outstanding teacher pre-service programs exemplified by the multimedia-based Remote Area Teacher Education Program for Indigenous teachers and the celebrated Bachelor of Learning Management (BLM), which focuses on the problem of teaching and its effects. Richard has had a long association with international education, cultural exchanges, and collaboration in Asia.

David Turner is Deputy Head of Research Projects in the Faculty of Education at Southern Cross University. He has enjoyed a diverse career in educational leadership as principal in a range of school communities and the tertiary sector as Head of Campus and Head of School, Learning and Innovation. David contributed to the development of leadership capabilities in Queensland schools for nearly a decade as Director of Professional Learning for a member-based school leader professional association. His knowledge and passion for professional learning have seen him present and consult nationally and internationally. David has published on topics such as the leadership mindsets necessary for a rapidly changing world and the need for schools to unleash the creative potential in all learners. He has worked as a member of research teams on projects related to initial teacher education, staff capability, and blended learning.

Barnett Berry has served in various academic and policy roles over his 40 year career to advance the teaching profession and a more equitable public education system. Currently, he works with the Learning Policy Institute, What School Could Be, and the University of Kansas's Center for Reimagining Education. Barnett's work in the 1990s with the National Commission on Teaching and America's Future led to his founding of the Center for Teaching Quality (CTQ) in 2000, and for 19 years the non-profit focused on igniting a bold brand of teacher leadership needed for students to lead their own learning. His two books, *TEACHING 2030* and *Teacherpreneurs* frame a bold vision for the profession's future. In 2021, Barnett was honoured by the National Board for Professional Teaching Standards with the James A. Kelly Award for Advancing Accomplished Teaching.

Jake Madden, an esteemed educator and author, has significantly contributed to the field of education through leadership, curriculum development, and teacher professional learning. He holds advanced degrees in education and leadership and has been at the helm of transformative change in schools across Australia and internationally. His work emphasises teacher capacity building and pedagogical restructuring, advocating for teachers as researchers to enhance student learning outcomes. Jake has authored several influential books, sharing his insights on educational excellence and innovation. Currently, he leads Aoba's schools in Tokyo, shaping future educational landscapes. Recognised globally, Jake's dedication to education continues to inspire and impact teachers and students worldwide.

David Spendlove is a Professor of Education at the University of Manchester, where he is Associate Dean in the Faculty of Humanities, currently leading on a major academic portfolio redevelopment. With expertise in education politics, David navigates the policy–practice intersection, drawing on an extensive background in leading initial teacher education. His impact extends internationally, contributing to research, policy, and curriculum development. Formerly a successful school leader, David transitioned into higher education and has participated in numerous national and international advisory and academic journal boards, offering insight based on significant experience and research in teacher development, assessment, curriculum design, and creative and design education.

Megan Lee is a Senior Teaching Fellow in the Faculty of Society and Design at Bond University in Australia. Megan specialises in education psychology and publishes research on student belonging, enjoyment, motivation and retention, the use of self-determined learning in teacher professional learning, and the impact of non-constructive commentary in student feedback surveys on academics' mental health. Megan also has expertise in research methods and qualitative and quantitative statistical analyses.

Part 1
The case for change

1   The teaching transformation agenda

An introduction

What's our key message?

- The education system is in need of a fresh perspective on schooling and teaching to address the challenges of a rapidly changing world.
- Education is a highly complex system requiring creativity and innovation to navigate effectively amid social change and competing interests.
- Many factors contribute to the resistance to change the education system, including tradition, lack of teacher agency and limited resources.
- There is a need for a transformational agenda in teaching and schooling, advocating for fundamental shifts rather than superficial adjustments.

Welcome to a book about our future that seeks to offer a fresh perspective on education, schooling, and teaching. A book we hope will assist the teaching profession in gaining its rightful place in a world that is now built on knowledge and a personal capacity to use and apply it. In articulating the positions presented and discussed in this book, we draw upon our collective experience in education as parents, teachers, school leaders, consultants, and academics. This experience includes having written countless articles and books on the topic and, importantly, having witnessed countless reviews in teaching, teacher education, and schooling, noting that these reviews have done little to advance the improvement agenda or the teaching profession. From observing years of what might be considered tinkering with a system beyond its use-by date, it is apparent that all that has resulted is increased layers of complexity, conformity, and accountability.

One realises when working in education that there are many moving parts with which to contend. Education is a highly complex system, and unlike complicated systems that pose problems that are technical in nature and offer opportunities for expertise to solve them, complexity brings ambiguity and usually requires creativity and innovation for breakthroughs to occur. When change is attempted, there are knock-on, unanticipated, and occasionally surprising effects in education. For example, include "new" content in initial teacher education, and students on

DOI: 10.4324/9781003303312-2

practicum may face mentor teachers who suggest they are now in the real world and should leave that academic guff outside the classroom. Undertake a curriculum review, and you unearth a multitude of interest groups arguing ferociously for the primacy of their positions. Change the operating hours of schools, and you realise how vital schools are for childminding. In the midst of it all, complexity manifests as frazzled and overworked classroom teachers who struggle with new societal expectations, a lack of consensus on how to react to social change, and a job that is becoming increasingly unattractive. So, you will read an expansive set of propositions in this book that are unfortunately located in a very complex set of circumstances. But you will also read about what we think is a fresh approach for dealing with education, schooling, teaching, and teacher education in a Knowledge Society context.

Let us start with questions that capture the challenges we have to contend with in writing this book. Why are some students in our schooling systems deemed to succeed and go on to realise their potential? Why is it so many do not? Why do some disengage and not seemingly try to reach their goals at all, even though they have the capacity to do so? Why is it, according to the Organisation for Economic Co-operation and Development (OECD, 2023), that almost 20% of students in developed countries don't complete Year 12? And why do some succeed in life despite their schooling experience? Is it just hard work and commitment that make the difference? Or is it because somebody, a teacher perhaps, fosters and develops an individual genius, instructs, mentors, encourages, or otherwise inspires a student to persist, to "give it a go", or to "hang in there" and build confidence about reaching their potential? Why does teaching no longer feature in the list of desired post-school studies today? Why is it the prevailing view that people study education to become schoolteachers when schools are not the only place where teaching and learning are conducted?

In this book, we seek to counter the complacency around these views by suggesting it is time for a transition to a new vision for education, the role of a teacher and how they are prepared, and how our schools are transformed to support the individual and collective capabilities necessary for the undetermined world to which we are heading. This book is advocating for new possibilities, perhaps against the odds. It is an attempt for a new approach to emerge from what is a contested space with a fresh insight into what it means to be "educated" and accordingly signal what must change to ensure the opportunity promised by schools for so long is a reality for all.

As we mentioned, all this is a complex set of circumstances. We have tried to present this book in a way that focuses the reader on what we think is important. We have been conscious of presenting a balanced view of things and covering what we think are important and key concepts. But as we say, it is a complex business, and we only have so many words to play with. In penning such a book, however, we hope to encourage the reader to think about things differently and seed a transformation and not more tinkering.

A changed world calling out for education's help

It is the end of the first quarter of the 21st century. Humanity is enmeshed in exponential technological and societal change that profoundly impacts how people live and how work is undertaken. At the centre of this change is a system of schooling that has hallmarks from an era now long past. As it has not adapted to these changes well, it now endures an ongoing and increasingly debilitating narrative that questions the effectiveness of schools and the work of teachers. Improving schools and teaching is now a preoccupation within our education systems.

There is a fundamental challenge in a world where there are clarion calls for improvement in our schools. Everyone has been to school and thus has an opinion on it. This should come as no surprise: Schooling, for all the good it has delivered, remains part of growing up, and tales abound in a multitude of individual experiences, personalities, aspirations, and circumstances, all mixed in a concoction of teaching and schooling traditions. This tradition suggests success at school is the key to a "better life": a life in which personal dreams and ambitions are realised. The argument goes that if you fail at school, your chances in life are severely curtailed. The gap between success and failure is magnified if you happen to be from a disadvantaged home, are non-English speaking, or have an Indigenous background. Schooling is thus the launching platform for life's awaiting journey, and people have a strong vested interest in it, especially if it is for their children. In addition, schooling is a seriously big business with nations investing significantly.

If you take a closer look at the world of schooling, you quickly realise that this utopian vision of educational opportunity for all is not as clear-cut as it should be. There is a well-trodden road of contested positions in what one could describe as a tug-of-war of viewpoints and ideologies. On one side, there is the argument that schools are failing our kids and that results do not warrant the investment made by the government. Our political masters and policymakers are spending enormous amounts on schools – without improvement. Schools are underperforming, apparently captured by out-of-step teachers, so it is time to acknowledge the evidence and make necessary changes. Teachers are critically implicated in all this and must change what they do! In this narrative, teacher unions are responsible for restrictive industrial practices and impediments to change and improvement. Teachers respond that they are overworked, the curriculum is overcrowded, there is too much testing and bureaucracy, and they must be left alone to do what they know is needed. A counter view is that it is a school funding issue and that the growing divide between private and public schools in regional, remote, and disadvantaged areas should be the focus of reform efforts. Here, too, countering views prevail. The way forward is increased spending on public education or corporatisation of schooling, letting market forces play their part. Then there is yet another view that suggests that the students and their parents are the problem. Individuality is king, and one's rights appear to trump any responsibility to the collective. Parents are busy and frazzled in their jobs and jump to complain when their precious child is not seen to be looked after and nurtured appropriately.

It is plain to see that work in schools is a hotbed of juggling competing demands and expectations. Then along comes a global pandemic, and schools are thrown into chaos as they are forced to close, students to learn from home, and teachers, many ill-prepared for the shift, are forced into teaching online. It is no wonder that for teachers who have been in the profession for some time and have experienced these changes, debates often hark back to the days of compliant kids, respectful parents, and quiet staffrooms.

Make no mistake, calls from governments worldwide are focused on improving teaching practices within their schools. These calls are loud, and the process is seemingly so drawn out that one could describe schools as being captured in a continuous cycle of institutionalised remediation as the competing views jostle for primacy. This is a disheartening situation, perhaps even demoralising, given the importance of a good education and the many years we have had to get schooling right. To imagine our hospital system in such a malaise is too tragic to comprehend. Nevertheless, schools remain caught in the status quo and are highly resistant to change.

Why is education so resistant to change?

The power of the status quo manifests in several ways and appreciating some of the forces at play is valuable at this point. We have identified five. First, it is crucial to appreciate that the task of changing schooling and, by direct association, teaching has been going on for decades. The problem is that the complexity of our education system inclines those engineering teaching improvement to do little more than tinker rather than transform. This is because the mindset of bringing about change is analogous to leaders of industry seeking to gain efficiencies on the production line in a factory. They see parts breaking down and needing repair rather than realising they are no longer fit for purpose. This Taylorism logic may have borne some results, small efficiencies, 50 or so years ago, but arguably ongoing "fixes" and countless system add-ons have made the task all the more difficult. Let us be upfront here and say that this is an issue of education system leadership but also about a lack of capacity for major change. By capacity, we mean teachers having the agency to respond, as part of their professional being, to effect change by being central to the strategy and not a victim of it. Our point is that teachers are not ready to do so – at least under the conditions in which most of them work – which brings us to the next reason education is resistant to change.

Second, the transformation agenda for schools requires significant shifts in how teachers are recruited, prepared, supported, and their work organised. It will require them, or at least some significant proportions, to become agents of change – "teacherpreneurs" (Berry et al., 2013) or "learning managers" (Smith & Moore, 2006). It will require policy leaders to find ways to break loose of education's past ways of working and for teachers to tell a new powerful story of their profession, re-establishing high levels of social capital with parents and the general public. But this is an enormous challenge as there are hundreds of thousands of teachers to engage in such change scenarios. Size does matter, and it will cost quite a bit. However, advancing technologies and forms of communicating, as well as the career expectations and new ideas from the more entrepreneurial proclivities of Generation Z teachers, might very well serve as catalysts to do just that, suggesting that we must rethink how we constitute this thing called a school.

Third, schooling as we know it in Western countries is steeped in tradition, with many long-standing practices and norms that have been in place for decades or even centuries. These traditions are deeply ingrained in the psyche of the teaching professional and how society views teachers. When all you have known is a "school as a school" and a "teacher in a classroom", conceptualising something new is not necessarily understood as required. Teachers have a well-founded, strong sense of professional identity and pride in their work, which can be a powerful motivator for maintaining the status quo. Being a highly unionised workforce also makes the change equation threshold higher. These circumstances make adopting new practices or approaches challenging as change threatens teachers' sense of identity and long-held and largely favourable industrial conditions. It is apparent then that change propositions to date have not engaged teachers to imagine or create a more exciting and improved world.

Fourth is the realisation that any schooling transformation process is fundamentally about the work of teachers. While there is an established body of research in education, it is by no means complete, and the translation of research findings into effective teaching practices, or even to inform a level of consensus on what should be accepted practice for the profession, seems not a high priority. Unlike medicine and nursing, which have a strong research-based practice culture that is doggedly fixed in codified practice, education is still grappling with how best to incorporate research into the process and business of education. Medicine has a more established evidence base, with research and clinical trials informing professional practices and treatment protocols, and medicine has and continues to attract far more research income than education, supported by the highly profitable pharmaceutical industry. In contrast, educational research can be less conclusive; it emerges from various research disciplines, making it subject to interpretation and thus not engendering a universally agreed position for implementation.

Fifth, schools often operate with limited resources, making it challenging to implement changes effectively. For example, implementing new technology or curriculum changes may require significant training, infrastructure, and equipment investments, which may not be feasible in all schooling contexts. Not to mention that technology is changing quickly, making keeping up challenging. Changing teaching is also expensive because teachers, due to the existing industrial model, have a designated group of young people in their care. This leaves little time during the workday for reskilling, retraining, or professional development. Any time away from teaching for professional learning or research is enabled only by employing another team of teachers to replace those who need to be engaged elsewhere. There is a chronic teacher shortage at the time of writing, making replacement increasingly difficult and impossible in some schools. However, any time off is often hijacked by some imposed policy position requiring immediate action and programming manoeuvring. This is another example showing that teacher agency and the capacity to enact change in the education system is practically non-existent.

To sum up, we are experiencing the emergence of a fundamentally different world. Not just technological innovation but climate change, social division, international conflict, and the growing divide between the "haves" and the "have nots" are causing a massive wave of social change that is washing over every aspect of our society, radically redefining how people think about their world, what is important and, most profoundly, how they choose to engage with it. In effect, this comes to represent the need for a fundamentally different set of schooling outcomes and a new set of success criteria. By invoking a call for new success criteria, we are not saying that all in the school curriculum should go, nor are we saying there is no such thing as "valid knowledge", nor that standards should be dropped, especially not concerning literacy and numeracy outcomes for students. We are saying that all this change signals that new success criteria are required to capture and reorientate the schooling experience to positions that better reflect this changing world logic and society's aspirations for all its young people. These circumstances demand a national conversation and resolution on what it means to be educated.

So why is a book like this needed?

By now, you should be getting a sense of why a book like this is needed, but let us delve deeper into the teaching improvement conundrum and see why we are motivated to write it. Pick up any newspaper, watch any news program, or read an education blog, and debates about the performance of our schools abound. Schools are being compared with schools in league tables; governments decry their education system's slide compared to other countries when they spend more on education; and parents are no longer content to choose the local school. Government leaders, especially in the West, call for schools to "improve" measured against global comparisons, and battles rage about what should and should not be taught in classrooms. It is a situation that is many decades in the making without, so it would seem, a resolution, as the following quotes suggest:

> Over the past two decades, despite a 60 per cent increase in real per-student funding, our school performance has gone backwards in absolute terms and versus other nations.
> Alan Tudge, education minister, Australia, 2020 to 2022 (Tudge, 2021)

> If we truly believe in our public schools, then we have a moral responsibility to do better – to break the either-or mentality around school reform and embrace a both-and mentality. Good schools will require both the structural reform and the resources necessary to prepare our kids for the future.
> Barack Obama, US President, 2009 to 2017 (Obama, 2006)

I'm clear that we do need to improve what's happening in our schools.
Michael Gove, Secretary of State for Education, UK, 2010 to 2014
(Gove, 2022)

Australia has a good education system, but it can be a lot better and fairer, and these results again highlight this.
Jason Clare, Minister for Education, Australia (Clare, 2023)

To understand why schooling systems have become national preoccupations is to appreciate this is in response to a system past its "use-by" date and a stubborn effort on the part of our system of education to continue to try to make it work. We must collectively examine the circumstances in which education occurs and redefine its purpose. We need to challenge our basic assumptions about schooling by looking carefully at its history, organisation, and the job of teaching. We need to challenge our current thinking about the role of public education as adolescents spend over eight hours a day in the virtual world, and artificial intelligence, including large language models like ChatGPT, are poised to make much of what kids do in school seem redundant. Then there has been the devastating impact of the COVID-19 pandemic, where sociologists are just beginning to document the miscellany of trauma, abuse, financial chaos, racial injustices, and political tribalism induced by it and which need to be addressed.

Over the last several decades, teaching improvement debates seem to toggle back and forth between teachers being able to teach as they see fit with little accountability and an environment of standardised testing and market-based mechanisms to cajole better teaching from teachers. The former allows for individual teacher autonomy and, at best, uneven student outcomes. The latter allows for identifying achievement gaps and performance issues but damped down teacher motivation and leadership. However, as Andy Hargreaves and Dennis Shirley noted 15 years ago, the old ways of advancing teaching and educational change are no longer suited to the fast, flexible, and volatile new world of the 21st century, and we are already one quarter into that century (Hargreaves & Shirley, 2009). We must confront the reality that just improving student outcomes in the old game of teaching and learning will stifle the prospects of many young people. It is time to change the game. The key message in this book is that we need a teaching transformation agenda, not more tinkering around the edges, hoping for improvement. So, let us begin a journey into understanding the complex world of education and reimagine how things could be much different and more attuned to the changing world we live in!

How the book is organised

A "key message" box heads each chapter to focus the reader on what will be explored. Correspondingly, an "agenda box" appears at each chapter's conclusion and acts to capture the emerging agenda for later chapter dealings. These inclusions are designed to focus you on a set of transformational ideas. The book is organised into four parts: in Part 1, we make the case for change. Chapter 2 examines the new socio-policy-education landscape and the repercussions for schools and teachers. In Chapter 3, we make the case that education systems are in crisis, and Chapter 4 explores what it means to be educated in this new world. In Part 2, we begin prefiguring changes to teaching, schooling, and teacher education. In Chapter 5, we do this by prefiguring what it means to be educated and building the case for new success criteria. Chapter 6 explores the concept of teaching transformation, and Chapter 7 presents a new school teaching logic. In Part 3, we begin designing a new paradigm for teaching and schooling, and Chapter 8 looks at new concepts for a transformation of teaching. Chapter 9 prefigures a new grammar of schooling, and Chapter 10 expands the focus for schools. In Chapter 11, we prepare a new teacher construct for a new grammar of schooling. In Chapter 12, we present a transformational teacher education program. Part 4 concludes our book in Chapters 13 and 14 by making critical final comments. Welcome to a book that aims to seed a new set of ideas for the important work captured by education, teaching, and schooling.

The teaching transformation agenda that is forming

- A need for creativity and innovation to transform schooling and teaching: not more tinkering.
- A call for a fresh approach in the context of a Knowledge Society to counter complacency and advocate for new possibilities.
- An importance of redefining the role of teachers, preparing them differently and transforming schools to support individual and collective capabilities.
- A need to confront challenges and foster a shift towards a more responsive and adaptable education system.

References

Berry, B., Byrd, A., & Wieder, A. (2013). *Teacherpreneurs: Innovative teachers who lead but don't leave*. Wiley.

Clare, J. (2023). *New report highlights importance of the next National School Reform Agreement*. https://ministers.education.gov.au/clare/new-report-highlights-importance-next-national-school-reform-agreement

Gove, M. (2022). *I'm clear that we need to improve what's happening in our schools*. www.quotetab.com/quote/by-michael-gove/im-clear-that-we-do-need-to-improve-whats-happening-in-our-schools

Hargreaves, A., & Shirley, D. (2009). *The fourth way: The inspiring future for educational change*. Corwin Press. https://doi.org/10.4135/9781452219523

Lynch, D. (2012). *Preparing teachers in times of change: Teaching school, standards, new content and evidence*. Primrose Hall Publishing Group. https://doi.org/10.53333/PRHPG/280209

Obama, B. (2006). *21st century schools for a 21st century economy*. http://obamaspeeches.com/057-21st-Century-Schools-for-a-21st-Century-Economy-Obama-Speech.htm

Organisation for Economic Co-operation and Development (OECD). (2023). *Education at a glance: OECD indicators.* www.oecd-ilibrary.org/sites/48e69087-en/index.html?itemId=/content/component/48e69087-en

Smith, R., & Moore, T. (2006). The learning management concept. In R. Smith & D. Lynch (Eds.), *The rise of the learning manager: Changing teacher education* (pp. 9–23). Pearson Education Australia.

Tudge, A. (2021). *Roaring back: My priorities for schools as students return to class.* https://ministers.dese.gov.au/tudge/roaring-back-my-priorities-schools-students-return-classrooms

2 A new world challenging schools and teachers

What's our key message?

- The current education system is not aligned with the demands of the Knowledge Society. Contested social circumstances complicate the teacher's work but can be resolved by a clarity of purpose for schooling.
- Social, economic, and political conditions are complicating teacher work. Technology is a huge challenge but a gigantic opportunity.
- Schools must adopt a broader, bolder approach to education. Education needs to develop in young people fundamentally different types of knowledges and skill sets.
- The education sector faces significant challenges, including technological advancements and societal changes. Schools alone cannot solve the problem.

In Chapter 1, we argued for the transformation of a system of education that is at odds with the Knowledge Society. The emergence of the Knowledge Society is a story of mounting challenges for our teachers, which appears to be overwhelming the profession today. In this chapter, we go deeper into the Knowledge Society to reveal its impacts on schools and identify the implications for those who teach. A starting point in understanding the challenge of transforming the work of teachers and the logic of schooling is to appreciate that teaching and learning today is a contested field, and it has been for what seems like forever. For example, there is no agreement about what constitutes quality teaching across jurisdictions, with significant variation evident in teacher standards internationally. A war of values, beliefs, programs, approaches, and theories is a constant distraction for practitioners, policy leaders, and the public from what evidence indicates matters. The bottom line is that the resolution to these contested elements can only start with a clarity of purpose for schooling. This is the foundation for transformation. Let us explain.

There is sufficient evidence to indicate that social, economic, and political conditions impact schools and the outcomes we want from them at any point in time. When further disruptions caused by climate change, catastrophes like warfare, a

DOI: 10.4324/9781003303312-3

global pandemic, or societal phenomena like the increasing mental health issues in our youth emerge, we add further uncertainties and complexity to the system of schooling. Even before the pandemic, one in five children in American public schools, for example, had a diagnosable mental illness, and this is apparent in countries such as Australia and England as well (Burke et al., 2016).

Many conditions inhibit a child's success at school and onwards that are beyond the school's capabilities to alter, but there are ways to establish renewed foundations of teaching and learning. Under the right conditions and organisational arrangements, schools can address the myriad of issues that impact with a broader and bolder approach to education. For example, when students are prepared across a broad range of knowledge, skills, abilities, and characteristics, they not only get better jobs, but they also engage more actively as citizens – especially in activities such as voting and community participation – which leads to a greater voice and influence in society. The task gets easier when various societal agencies join forces for the common good (Broader Bolder Approach to Education, 2023). Our key point is that schools, as they are currently designed and organised for teacher work, cannot alone deliver on ensuring that every young person has developed the complex set of skills and competencies that ready them for careers and civic life. A new model of what a school is and what the teacher does within them is now required.

Over the last several decades, a no-excuses approach to school reform has become familiar policy rhetoric. This is evidenced by the rise of charter schools in the United States and academies in England. We explore these approaches in the next chapter. Some of the "no-excuses schools" in the United States have produced improved test scores through strict disciplinary procedures and tight adherence to instructional methods like direct instruction, in which novice teachers focus intently on a narrow set of academic skills. Stressed students and a revolving door of recruits to teaching have become commonplace. Please do not misinterpret what we are saying here. We are not making the case against adequate instructional time, targeted instruction, structured pedagogy, as well as teachers and school leaders committed to "no excuses for failure" and who are informed about pedagogical strategies that have credible research foundations. These and the general ambience of schools are irrevocably connected to the structures that support students. They are also enabled or disrupted by influences outside the school.

However, people in the education system know, intuitively, that schools and teaching have remained static for generations despite waves of social change sweeping over them. While many contemporary classrooms have all manner of modern inclusions, the reality is that the rationale and the modus operandi for what goes in classrooms have not changed much for 200 years: age-related groupings, standardised school days, knowledge acquisition by discipline, success measured by standardised tests. Parades, formal salutations, and other traditions persist. While recognisable to previous generations who have gone to school, at least in the West, this static profile is incongruent with the changes in today's globally interconnected society moulded by technological innovation. We acknowledge that there have been many attempts at repositioning our schools and the work of teachers. However, arguably, the impacts have been minimal and have often contributed to polarising debates and increased complexity. So, something needs to change!

Furthermore, tumultuous political and economic conditions – the pandemic, global warming, racial unrest, and deepening generational divides – create powerful structural and cultural changes that challenge the meaning of education and the teaching profession. What may appear to be irresistible forces for change in the education system and what to do about them may be largely imperceptible to many political leaders. It is a central theme running throughout this book. While many policy and education leaders and parents want schools to improve, too few seem to want them to look any different than when they were at school. Predictions about change in education are nothing new and perhaps a fool's game for many. Nevertheless, we can identify "loose bricks" and "weak signals" in the present with the knowledge that forward thinking is preferable to crisis management. The latter is generally an attempt to recover what is left of the wreckage rather than a good outcome for individuals, communities, and societies. Bricks and signals are already determining the shape of education, albeit in important or even dangerous ways, as they force education systems to accommodate forces beyond their control or become redundant. Let us now examine some of these loose bricks and weak signals.

Liberalism under pressure

In the last 200 years in Western countries, the dominant political philosophy has been a broad consensus in favour of "liberalism". Belief in and institutionalisation of legal equality for all adult citizens, respect for evidence, reason and diversity in opinions, separation of state and church, freedom of religion, limitations on government power, universal human rights, and political democracy have shaped the way of life. The system of belief in these ideals applied to all individuals, imperfect as they are, has overcome slavery and colonialism and decisively opposed fascism, communism and other authoritarian right and left systems. Nevertheless, they are under pressure not just to be modified but extinguished. Today, liberalism as a system of ideas is under pressure from both right-wing populist movements, seeking strong leaders to protect them against declining living standards and what they perceive as progressive policies, and left-wing authoritarianism that rejects liberal values and institutions as oppressive. "Identity politics", which appears in the media daily, is the face of the "culture war" struggle between liberalism and competing values and political stances. The effects on education are apparent at all levels and have not yet played out.

A typical teaching approach in schools, "constructivism" – a theory built around the idea that learners construct knowledge by experiencing the world and incorporating new information into pre-existing knowledge – has resulted from such pressures despite contrary indications. Constructivist approaches to teaching and learning are said to begin with the student's needs, interests, abilities, and talents, and contribute to other primary educational goals, such as creativity, critical thinking, motivation, self-awareness, and more. In contrast, critics point out that constructivism in education is deeply implicated in the seemingly intractable gap of education achievement, according to standardised tests of academic knowledge, and its consequential effects on the life chances of the least advantaged that characterise Western countries.

For critics of constructivism, schools and teachers are to teach the basics; learners do not need to construct the ideas of potential energy, mutation, photosynthesis, and fractions for themselves. Teachers must explain these ideas to students in ways they know and show they do. In *The Tyranny of Merit: What's Become of the Common Good?* Michael Sandel (2021) argues that attempts to perfect educational meritocracy without questioning its foundational assumptions generate hubris among the winners and the harsh judgement of those left behind. Our workplaces in schools and universities – our main professional interests in teacher (and school leader) preparation – are central players in these struggles. Schools can either offer much-needed pathways to the liberation of oppressed people by revealing hidden biases and assumptions inherited from the past and institutionalised in modernist liberal structures and cultures or can be seen as an accelerator of political correctness that some believe should not be taught in schools. Teach just the basics – say some political leaders – and leave the values to be taught at home.

However, depending on one's view, the underlying theories of postmodernism and Critical Theory that have become orthodox in our universities now dominate the focus of teacher educators. In education, cancel culture, school closure, language changes, gender changes, decolonising the curriculum, and so on that are mostly framed as morally necessary and undebatable pose fundamental threats to education and society (Gutentag, 2022).

Technology and the challenges to education as we know it

Silicon Valley startups have already begun to re-engineer education delivery for the online era. Online lessons, projects, lectures, readings, teacher's notes, blogs, and standardised tests are already available to provide access to education worldwide and reduce delivery costs through potential massive scaling. Such "digital Taylorism" holds the tantalising prospect for some constituencies of partly replacing the complex institution of schooling (nursing, legal services, and even teachers) sooner rather than later. Increasingly capable artificially intelligent robots and computer systems have already created industrial reorganisation and technological change that removes low-skilled, manual labour, and mid-skill jobs. At the present rate of development, many white-collar and probably entire professions are likely to disappear as structural unemployment gathers pace.

Income inequality between those with the gold-standard education qualifications and those without has already been felt in education. More affluent families with considerable economic, social, and cultural resources could always use education and dominate high-status employment, which underscores social divisions (Rivera, 2015). Income inequality and national political struggles are intertwined in the social environment of education, and it can be expected that education will have a high political profile for the rest of this decade and beyond, just as it has in the past. We show later how fundamental changes at the school level can disrupt this process.

The Futurist David Tal (2020) emphasises the labour market's effects on education, where artificial intelligence (AI)-powered machines and computers will eventually consume or make obsolete up to 47% of today's jobs. He argues that it is advantageous, indeed essential, for education to produce polymaths. He advocates preparation in the STEM body of knowledge and skills together with the humanities for teaching and fostering social skills and creative and critical thinking. Preparation of the young for the transdisciplinary requirements of tomorrow's labour market and the kinds of social behaviours and transversal skills needed in changed workplaces underpins this view. Microsoft officials note that because of our extensive exposure to the web, the average attention span has shrunk to 8 seconds today, compared to 12 seconds in 2000 (Southern California Public Radio, 2015). In addition, our minds are less able to explore complex topics and memorise large amounts of data. However, they are far more adept at switching between many different topics and activities and thinking non-linearly. This reflects traits computers are better at and traits related to abstract thought with which computers currently struggle. The rapid development of AI will undoubtedly deal with this obstacle if it has not already, and perhaps the implication is that school teaching as we know it has already become obsolete.

The future approach to education correctly draws attention to technological possibilities and their focus on vocational skills rather than solely on the academic. One can understand that in an era of increasing income differentials, structural unemployment, and social division, getting a good job has become the purpose of public education. With the accelerating cost of university education and the transformation of the global economy, the humanities, when mentioned, appear to be the medium for getting to technological vocational ends rather than having value in themselves. Others, like education professor and author Richard Pring (2011), believe that the cultural resources and primary purpose of the arts and humanities provide the stimulus for raising those questions of deep concern to young people: what does it mean to be human? Technological advocates seem to avoid those endless conversations about the purposes of education. We must remind ourselves repeatedly that the popular political claim about education promoting public goods for national goals and global competitiveness is not an educational argument but a statement of values. This and many other associated values affect fundamental curriculum choices made by the full range of education designers in the technological age.

Take the idea that knowledge acquisition is outmoded. The glib line that "knowledge can be just looked up on Google" is countered by the fact that Google routinely censors knowledge, making it a relatively worthless source of knowledge for educational purposes, especially in social justice and other now controversial perspectives. Similarly, catchy lines such as education is about the "acquisition of skills" for the future and what is commonly called the "Four Cs":

communication, creativity, critical thinking, and collaboration in the curriculum are, according to author and education blogger Bri Stauffer (2021), needing proper evaluation. It is unclear how one "thinks" about these four skill elements without prior knowledge. Again, critical thinking can be learnt, but it is "quite difficult, and it can take a long time to master", according to a substantial 2015 meta-analysis of the research (Zarvana, 2020).

"Critical thinking" in this sense would seem wishful thinking hyperbole in the social justice environment because it is the effect of expert knowledge in particular fields, many of which postmodern education advocates reject. The detail in the prognostications must be unpacked against the background where dissenting views are shut down. Teachers do not teach students critical thinking as another content standard to meet and assess. Instead, these so-called soft skills of the Four Cs are cultivated in how teachers teach and students are expected to learn.

Reforming teaching and schooling today cannot avoid an emphasis on educating students to develop those skills in which computers don't appear to excel, such as social skills, creative thinking, and transdisciplinary skills, rather than repetition, memorisation, and calculation. Regarding the latter, computers are supreme, and not so much regarding the former. The silence in this line of thinking is that appropriate knowledge precedes these powerful concepts. Not all students have such a background in schools, leaving them vulnerable to exclusion when the stakes are higher. Increasing numbers of people will possess some qualifications and skills in the hope that they will advance in the meritocracy of societies such as Australia, England, and the United States. Not all will succeed in the present arrangements. However, educational reform continues to be dichotomised – it is one thing versus another. Rarely both. Moreover, even more unusual, "third-way" thinking can be found. The third way is the middle-ground alternative route to socialism and free-market capitalism.

The great online learning experiment

As we emerge from the global pandemic struggle where government actions around the virus and their "scientific" advice have disrupted the lives of just about everyone – tragically, lives lost for many – it seems that many social changes have taken place. However, for our purposes here, the most significant is that for many parents, Zoom, and homeschooling notes provided a periscope view of public and private school classrooms like never before. Most were probably relieved that there was some guidance for mums and dads who, by necessity, were asked to perform what the teaching profession maintains is a difficult professional task – teaching in engaging ways that motivate children to learn. The adequacy of supportive materials and the approaches to lessons and curriculum content exposed parents to the kind of professional educational monoculture that teachers, principals, school governance boards, teachers' unions, and academic schools of education share. In the ensuing Twitter and Facebook traffic, media coverage, and word of mouth, parents saw what and how their kids were being taught, and from what we saw, they wanted to know more.

Ferri et al. (2020) reveal three sets of post-COVID-19 educational challenges: technological, pedagogical, and social. Technologically, the restricted availability of devices and non-existent or inadequate internet connections proved to be constraints. The lack of interactive multimedia teaching materials that engage and motivate students was apparent. Pedagogically, teachers' lack of skills in using technology to implement credible online pedagogical processes and the need for training, teaching, and content guidelines for teachers and their students were revealed. Student feedback and evaluation systems were found wanting as well. In short, the standard teacher education assumptions and practices needed a makeover. Socially, one of the main limitations of online teaching was the loss of human interaction between teachers and students and among students. Significantly, although the use of ICT gadgets is like an extended arm for students worldwide who feel comfortable with them, there is no substitute for proper teacher–student interaction. While the forum report suggested that online teaching can complement face-to-face lessons, it was clear that not all activities can be done online. It seemed that educators had even more proof that relationships matter in school learning.

COVID-19 seemed, at least for a while, to have "frozen" school reform, creating indisputable tumult in teaching and learning. The effects of the pandemic on education offer an unprecedented opportunity to rethink and rebuild a "science" of teaching relevant to the emerging education environment, which would benefit all students.

The policy aim we maintain without prevarication should be a national priority. An interplay of these three issues, which we think will determine the future of education, are touch points in later chapters of this book. We have no illusions that they will be definitively solved once and for all and that we have all the answers. Moreover, we know that in taking on such issues head-on, we will face strong opposition and derision from the education orthodoxy. We also will face pushback from those who seek to monetise public education. We are for thinking outside the box and proposing new ways to get around those major education obstacles to closing the achievement gap that impacts so many individuals and communities and the grandiose plans of politicians. Education has been a contested field – and we suspect it always will be. We must deal with it.

Noel Pearson (2006), an Australian Indigenous icon and national intellectual, speaking from what life is like "down in the Marianas Trench of disadvantage", argues that "it is too early" to give up on the classical ideal that educational improvement "can take place despite socio-economic disadvantage", Similarly, Piketty (2017) supports investment in education to reduce social inequality. We suspect that most parents who still see education as an investment in the future would endorse this view, believing that their children will stand or fall by the quality of the education they receive in government or private schools and post-school institutions. The challenge of this book is to show how that goal can be implemented. Our words have located and explained a set of concerns that lie at the heart of what one can call the "challenge of modern-day schooling and education". These concerns have identified things that now require a sense of well-argued resolution. This is important because, as we outlined earlier, personal success in the modern technological global world goes hand in hand with a fit-for-purpose schooling system, where questions arise such as "What does it mean to be educated?" and correspondingly "How is this best done?"

The teaching transformation agenda that is forming

- A need to define the purpose of education amid mounting challenges and contested ideologies, aiming to align teaching and learning with the evolving demands of the Knowledge Society.
- A broader, bolder approach addressing diverse issues impacting students' success through collaborative efforts involving various societal agencies.
- Re-evaluation and repositioning of schools and teaching methods to better prepare students for future challenges.
- Rethinking teaching practices, leveraging technology, and fostering meaningful teacher–student interactions to ensure educational relevance and effectiveness in the modern era.

References

Broader Bolder Approach to Education. (2023). *A broader, bolder approach to education.* www.boldapproach.org

Burke, M. P., Martini, L. H., Çayır, E., Hartline-Grafton, H. L., & Meade, R. L. (2016). Severity of household food insecurity is positively associated with mental disorders among children and adolescents in the United States. *The Journal of Nutrition*, 146(10), 2019–2026. https://doi.org/10.3945/jn.116.232298

Ferri, F., Grifoni, P., & Guzzo, T. (2020). Online learning and emergency remote teaching: Opportunities and challenges in emergency situations. *Societies*, 10(4), 86. https://doi.org/10.3390/soc10040086

Gutentag, A. (2022). *The new authoritarians.* www.tabletmag.com/sections/news/articles/new-authoritarians

Halpern, D. F. (2013). *Thought and knowledge: An introduction to critical thinking.* Psychology Press.

Pearson, N. (2006). *Layered identities and peace.* https://parlinfo.aph.gov.au/parlInfo/search/display/display.w3p;query=Id:%22media/pressrel/MPDK6%22

Piketty, T. (2017). *Capital in the twenty-first century.* Belknap Press.

Pring, R. (2011). Can education compensate for society. *Forum*, 53(1). https://journals.lwbooks.co.uk/forum/vol-53-issue-1/article-4569/

Rivera, L. A. (2015). *Pedigree: How elite students get elite jobs.* Princeton University Press. https://doi.org/10.2307/j.ctv7h0sdf

Sandel, M. J. (2021). *The tyranny of merit: What's become of the common good?* Penguin Press.

Southern California Public Radio. (2015). *Microsoft attention spans research report.* www.scribd.com/document/265348695/Microsoft-Attention-Spans-Research-Report

Stauffer, B. (2021). *What are the 4 C's of 21st century skills?*www.aeseducation.com/blog/four-cs-21st-century-skills

Tal, D. (2020). *Future of teaching, future of education.* www.quantumrun.com/prediction/future-teaching-future-education-p3

Zarvana. (2020). *Critical thinking can be learned: Here's the evidence-based way how.* www.zarvana.com/blog/critical-thinking-can-be-learned-heres-the-evidence-based-way-how%2F

3 Education systems in crisis

What's our key message?

- Socio-technological changes disrupt modern society, prompting governments to question the efficacy of education systems.
- Australia's education landscape includes ongoing reviews, funding complexities, and tension between state and federal control.
- England's education system faces challenges like Brexit, government instability, and a move towards academisation, impacting teaching approaches.
- In the United States, public schooling history reveals inequalities, while teachers navigate reforms, high-stakes accountability, and social pressures.

In Chapter 2, we identified a set of circumstances conspiring to complicate teachers' work and schools' business. At its heart is a rapidly evolving set of socio-technological changes disrupting all aspects of modern society. In response, governments of all persuasions have recognised the importance of a high-quality education system. Taking reference from international education assessment regimes, such as the OECD's Program for International Student Assessment (PISA) (OECD, 2023), together with clarion calls for schools to deal with an ever-increasing range of issues, they are questioning the efficacy of their education systems. The increasing investment in education and the apparent lack of commensurate improvement further spur them into action. This action invariably means rounds of reviews and reports, followed by significant attempts at restructuring. In this chapter, we explore the government's actions in Australia, England, and the United States as a case study to reveal an education landscape that tells a familiar story: education, schooling, and teaching are in some kind of crisis. We focus on these three countries because we work in these education contexts as authors, but also because they exemplify what is happening in most Western countries. Let us begin our exploration by examining what is happening in Australia.

DOI: 10.4324/9781003303312-4

The Australian context

Australia is a large island continent with a relatively small population that administers education through its eight states and territories. These jurisdictions have operational control of their public schools, set education and curriculum delivery policies, and employ teachers. These arrangements are initially a product of the country's federation. However, increasingly complex arrangements for school funding resulted from reforms over many decades when new legislation provided government funding to religious schools in 1964. Today, the Australian schooling ecosystem funds, with public money, three schooling systems: a fully public one that accounts for approximately 64% of students, a Catholic one with just under 20% of students, and a range of independent schools with 16% of enrolments. The latter may be part of smaller systems, such as church or affiliated, or be fully independent. The Catholic and independent sectors are bolstered financially through the capacity of charging school fees. This can cost as much as $50,000 a year in the most exclusive schools.

In recent years, there have been moves to centralise the development of curriculum and the regulation of teaching, school leadership, and teacher education through various agreements and the establishment of statutory bodies. These include the Australian Institute of Teaching and School Leadership (AITSL, 2005) and the Australian Curriculum Assessment and Reporting Authority (ACARA, 2008), responsible for a national curriculum, assessment, and reporting. The reality is that there is a tension between state and territory rights to determine education in their jurisdiction and the federal government's desire for national education quality and value-for-money educational outcomes.

The Australian education landscape can be characterised by an ongoing set of public reviews and reports into the quality of teaching, the performance and cost of schools, and the relevance of teacher education programming, which have occurred with monotonous regularity over the past four decades or so. For example, the Schools Commission Act (1973) introduced needs-based funding into the education system, while the Melbourne Declaration on Educational Goals for Young Australians (Barr, 2008) set out a national vision for education, emphasising the importance of equity, excellence, and preparing students for the 21st century. The Gonski Review (2011) called for another new needs-based funding model. These reviews occurred in the context of ongoing debates about what should be in the curriculum, what should be removed, and whether the nation should have one curriculum instead of one for each state and territory. At the time of writing, these debates continue.

While schools and teachers have had their fair share of reviews and reports, teacher education has come in for the most criticism. Over the past 40 years, every successive federal government has reviewed teacher education, made scathing remarks about its outcomes, and enacted policy and regulatory changes in vain attempts to reorientate what is primarily a university offering in Australia. The nation has witnessed, for example (to name just a few), the Teacher Education Review (1981), resulting in recommendations for improvements in curriculum, practicum experiences, and admission standards for teacher education courses; the Ministerial Council on Education, Employment, Training and Youth Affairs Taskforce on Teacher Quality (2003) to address teacher quality and identify the need for improvements in teacher education programs, including increased subject knowledge and improved pedagogical skills and the Teacher Education Ministerial Advisory Group (TEMAG) Review (2014) to address concerns about the quality of initial teacher education, making recommendations to improve selection criteria, strengthen practical experience, and enhance accreditation processes. The Teacher Education Expert Panel (TEEP; 2023) once again criticised teacher education but ramped up the rhetoric on reform by mandating key study elements and foreshadowing performance penalties.

While reviews have been characteristic of the education governance and policy environment, a chronic shortage of teachers in all areas of the country and most teaching areas, coupled with high levels of attrition, teacher complaints about heavy workloads, poor student behaviour and poor pay, and conditions have been a constant narrative in the national media. At the time of writing, the current federal Labor government is renegotiating its funding compact with state education jurisdictions, arguing for improved teaching and learning outcomes, signalling yet more government interventions in the national education system.

The English context

At the time of writing, teachers in England are currently on strike for the first time in many years. While partly about pay, the strikes are also being framed as "education in crisis" (National Education Union, 2023) due to workload and an increasing recruitment and retention problem that ultimately have an impact on a teacher's wellbeing and children's education. While the extent of the problem should not be understated, the realities are that the complexities of maintaining and developing a teaching workforce, educating a nation to "higher standards", and set within a context of ever-changing economic and political uncertainties mean these are familiar challenges that education jurisdictions around the world face. However, within the context of England, the current crisis can be further framed around the simultaneous and perhaps unique impacts of:

- Exit from the European Union (following Brexit), alongside conflict in Ukraine.
- Government instability resulting in an unprecedented five different secretaries of state for education across 2022.
- Significant policy reform across the last decade within a context of increasing teacher recruitment and retention difficulties.
- A widening attainment gap between the poorest and most "advantaged" in society.

The consequences of the above challenges mean that the context for navigating and understanding the teaching transformation agenda has become more complex and will be explored in further detail. However, from the outset, a point of clarification is required to explain why the focus is on England and not the United Kingdom (UK).

Since the 1988 Education Reform Act, there has been a proliferation of policies from all political parties linked to increasing competition, marketisation, and accountability. Perhaps the most significant development has been moving away from local democratic governance and control of schools through Local Education Authorities (LEAs) to semi-independent schools in the form of academisation, based on the public charter school model in the United States. In particular, the academisation of schools over the last decade has accelerated significantly, with approximately 80% of state secondary schools (for pupils 11–16 or 11–18) now an academy, albeit with a lower rate of conversion for primary schools (for students aged 5–11) at around 40%. The longer-term ambition is that all state schools will become academies as part of Multi-Academy Trusts (MATs), with many MATs likely to operate locally within a school network. However, the optimum size and make-up of MATs is seen to be around 10–15 schools, offering sufficient capacity to benefit from economies of scale. Likewise, larger, national MATs, consisting of over 20 schools and representing around 10% of MATs, are less common but are often seen as highly influential in policy and practice given their critical mass and strategic importance.

The simplistic premise of academies and MATs is that through structural reform and direct funding from the government, LEAs can be bypassed to raise standards in academies through a combination of autonomy, competition, marketisation, and corporatisation. Furthermore, MATs can also have sponsors from businesses, universities, or faith groups, which contributes to blurring the lines between public and private ownership and the values that schools may have. For example, ARK (Absolute Return for Kids) academies have a network of 39 schools founded by hedge fund managers who correspondingly have increasing political and policy influence within England's education system. While business efficiencies and economies of scale may be of value to networks of schools, difficulties inevitably emerge when attempting to broker sponsorship for the "least successful" schools. In such circumstances, "challenging schools", which may serve areas of dis-advantage, become a liability and less attractive due to being resource intensive while carrying reputational damage to potential sponsors where the "perfor-mance" of a school might be considered low. Therefore, "failing schools" can become "orphan schools" or SNOWs (schools no one wants) due to a system built on a commercial model that views success by a limited set of metrics. Like-wise, parental wishes and local expertise can also be bypassed, where the chain of schools crosses geographical boundaries and adopts a corporate approach across the school chain. In such circumstances, admissions criteria can equally promote exclusive rather than inclusive approaches, presenting challenges to diverse stu-dents or students with special educational needs.

"Free schools" have also emerged as a further strand of the government strategy across the last decade. However, ironically, the 600-plus schools are far from "free" as they typically cost more to operate. These schools are a further type of academy but have additional freedoms, including the freedom to set their pay, with a key difference being that they are set up from scratch rather than converted from an existing school as with the general academies. As such, start-up costs can

be high due to the innovation aspect of free schools; they do not have to repro-
duce the existing norms around school buildings, curriculum, and staffing. A further distinctive feature of free schools is that they are "set up in response to what
local people say they want and need in order to improve education for children in
their community", with the evident irony being that free schools have the local
voice which LEAs used to have, and which has been denied in many academies
(United Kingdom Department for Education, 2015).

It can, therefore, be seen that within a relatively short period, primarily across
the last decade, the emergence of a highly fragmented school system was accelerated by the Conservative government through a desire to impose market principles
on the school system, with little understanding of the likely consequences of rapid
policy reform. Despite such changes being framed as addressing social justice
issues, the attainment gap between the poorest and most advantaged has been at
the broadest level for a decade. Likewise, the "evidence on whether or not academies have had more success in raising attainment than other equivalent schools
is mixed and hard to pin down" (Linford, 2015). Such little movement in
addressing the baked-in disadvantage confirms that structural reform alone, a significant strategy of successive governments culminating in new types of schools,
does not lead to sustained improvement.

The use of metrics to influence schools through additional accountability has
been a feature of successive governments since the introduction of Standard
Attainment Tests (SATs) in the late 1980s alongside the introduction of a national
curriculum. With the emergence of national tests at ages 5, 7, 11, and 14, followed by formal GCSE examinations at 16 and further advanced examinations at
ages 17 and 18, England's students and schools became one of the world's most
tested nations. Tests were used as performance measures with league tables com-
paring and increasing school competition. However, while the format and fre-
quency of SATs may have changed, the use of high-stakes assessments and
performance measures, which now include early years foundation (ages 4 to 5)
baseline profiling within the first weeks of school, are repeatedly seen to distract
and distort teaching from core activities. This is further exemplified by the introduction of the English Baccalaureate (EBacc), a performance measure for schools
based on student entries and performance in five areas: English Language,
Mathematics, Science, Humanities, and Languages. A consequence of the implementation of this forced "grammar school curriculum", under the pretence of
increasing access to "elite universities", has meant a 40% drop in arts subjects in
state schools since 2010 (The Guardian, 2023).

While the increased focus on assessment metrics has had a profound and dis-
torting impact on schools, the most significant influence in shaping the teaching
"improvement" agenda has undoubtedly come from the Office for Standards in
Education, Children's Services and Skills (Ofsted). The non-ministerial department is meant to be impartial, operating "without fear or favour" and independent of government, but it has become increasingly inseparable from policy while
maintaining a significant blind spot as to its limitations and at the same time
holding others to account for circumstances beyond their control. Through

Ofsted's role of regulating, inspecting, and publicly reporting school performance, it has increasingly shaped and prioritised how and what schools should teach. Consequently, through public reporting and grading of schools, naming and shaming, its influence has frequently been recognised as potentially causing more harm than good. However, its role in leveraging policy on behalf of the government means the government values its influence. However, the adverse effects of the public degrading of schools and teachers and the significance of Ofsted's grading of schools means that schools remain "preoccupied" with being "Ofsted ready". Schools will mostly receive less than 24 hours' and sometimes as little as 15 minutes' notice of an inspection (Ofsted, 2023).

The stakes involved in Ofsted inspections have consequently become incredibly high. For example, schools judged as "inadequate" can be forced to either become an academy or to join an alternative academy trust. Schools deemed "outstanding" can "benefit" from increased competition from parents wanting their children to attend such a school even though the use, accuracy, and reliability of grading of schools is recognised as flawed. However, such is the hype around a school's grade that house prices near "outstanding" schools have also been shown to be significantly higher than those near lower-rated schools, paradoxically impacting those who can afford to live within an "outstanding" school's catchment area.

Ofsted's grading of schools further distorts the performative nature of schools through both narrowing the curriculum and the way teachers teach. Over the last two decades, Ofsted's "preferred" teaching methods significantly changed and influenced teachers from a period where group work was prioritised to the current vogue of "knowledge-rich" and shallow interpretation of cognitive science. Consequently, teacher agency is removed as schools, often as part of MATs, manage the high-stakes accountability through implementing what are seen as best-bet teaching approaches deemed successful in navigating likely Ofsted inspections. Ultimately, the surveillance culture that Ofsted has created has stifled the profession, with the narrow prescriptive view of "effective teaching" prevailing, which now extends to the pre-service and professional development of teachers and the marginalising of the "independent" autonomous voice of universities by the government. Prior to the 2010 change of government, there was a move towards a master's degree profession; however, since then, almost all teacher professional development has moved away from universities, often to government-funded organisations that give the appearance of being independent while working to a government agenda, or to MATs who may have an additional designation as "teaching schools".

Within pre-service education, while university providers have performed exceptionally well on all key performance measures, the government has been determined to increase control over initial teacher education (ITE) content while increasing providers' accountability. As such, a similar short-notice Ofsted inspection (48 hours) exists for ITE providers, along with the grading of providers, which has equally distorted the practice of ITE. Likewise, despite a significant amount of time (approximately a minimum of two-thirds) spent in the classroom "training" to be a teacher, alongside a solid commitment to subject knowledge and pedagogy, and despite being built upon a robust partnership model where schools and universities work closely to integrate theory and practice, the government has sought to marginalise universities through a reaccreditation system which had little to do with the quality or effectiveness of provision. Those unwilling or unable to convince the Department for Education of their allegiance to their plans for new content and structure of ITE have subsequently failed their accreditation, with 12 universities with a long tradition of ITE losing their accreditation. This is despite having previously navigated the challenges of adapting provision over the last decade that have required diversifying provision, implementing increased marketised approaches, and meeting the demands of multiple Ofsted inspection frameworks with differing priorities.

Inevitably, within England's education system, with its five-year terms of government, there is inescapable exposure to the fragilities of the prevailing political priorities. Within the context of a teaching improvement agenda, this has seen a move away from progressive education towards a neo-traditional and neoliberal view of education based on an emphasis on behaviour and knowledge-rich approaches. As such, a culture war exists, based around a binary of progressive versus traditional forms of schooling, teaching, and assessment. The premise of an evidence-based approach to teaching has been central to these developments; however, university voices have been marginalised and constrained, with only certain forms of research being considered valid while an equally narrow view of evidence is often drawn upon.

Ultimately, teachers' agency is being eroded as a limited palette of evidence is used to constrain rather than liberate teachers within an increasingly marketised, micromanaged, and hyper-surveillance system. Equally, while the system attempts to self-correct through faux critique of different forms of elitism, it inevitably achieves the opposite by sustaining and reproducing exclusivity within a class-based culture. Within this context, the current path of de-professionalising teachers is set to continue, partly due to the political will not being able or willing to sustain a highly educated and well-paid workforce alongside a determination by the government to increasingly prescribe and proscribe content and pedagogy. This "technicising" of teaching is therefore achieved through marginalising the intellectual basis of teaching by diminishing the contribution of universities, increasing competition between schools, and "outsourcing" professional development into organisations that give the appearance of being respectfully benign yet are contractually coerced to "deliver" content in line with policy. Consequently, disparities between "rich and poor" pervade, and inequity remains as entrenched as ever.

The US context

Understanding the teaching transformation agenda in the United States requires a quick dive into the history of public education and the profession itself. Since the nation's founding, public schooling, whose mission was to prepare students for democracy, has not been accessible to everyone. Many children have been excluded based on race or ethnicity, gender, and other factors. America's journey in offering high-quality, universal public education has been gradual and uneven. The US Constitution does not mention education and, as a result, public schooling is quite decentralised, with the states and local communities having the most influence on critical decisions – including what is taught and by whom. Since the mid-20th century, the federal government has focused on promoting equity in public schooling. However, even today, it only accounts for around 10% of spending on educating approximately 50 million students in 13,000 school districts (National Centre for Education Statistics, 2023).

The "anatomy of inequality" in US public education is anchored in inequalities in the community, including the highest rates of child poverty in the industrialised world. In addition, schools serving the most vulnerable children tend to be chronically short of teachers who have the knowledge and skill as well as the working conditions needed to teach them in developmentally appropriate, culturally responsive ways. The roots of US public education – what it taught and how it is assessed – also remain grounded in Fredrick Taylor's early 20th-century theories of scientific management used to jumpstart output in American assembly-line factories, and in the ideas of Edward Thorndike, a pre-eminent educational psychologist who believed that most students had limits on what they could learn and that learning was incremental and linear. A grammar of schooling – separating classes by academic discipline, age grading of classrooms, and assessing results through standardised tests – has been built to efficiently march students through assembly-line learning of pre-existing knowledge – and dominates the what and how of US public education (Tyack & Cuban, 1995). John Dewey, the icon of more progressive education where students follow their passions in learning, not just focusing on academic skills but also those needed for life in a democracy, has enormously influenced American education. However, as Raymond Callahan noted over 60 years ago, "American schools have been built on a cult of efficiency" (Callahan, 1962, p. 49).

Despite the lack of a centralised anything in American education, the use of high-stakes accountability and the grading of schools based on standardised student achievement tests doubled down on more Thorndike approaches to teaching and learning. The federal No Child Left Behind Act (NCLB) of 2002, signed into law by Republican President George Bush, was a well-intentioned piece of bipartisan legislation with the primary aim of focusing schools' attention on improving test scores for all groups of students, providing parents with more educational choices, and ensuring better-qualified teachers. However, 20 years after the law's enactment, little positive evidence of its impact can be found.

In American schools, the cult of efficiency remains clear and present. As Linda Darling-Hammond has noted of late:

> Our current school system has been anchored in the belief that only some students are worthy of investment – and that students need to be ranked and sorted according to their potential – is deeply rooted in the organisational design of our schools, our funding priorities, our testing and grading policies, and our systems for tracking and labelling students.
>
> (Darling-Hammond, 2022)

Americans never seem to agree on the goals of public schooling – whether in 1925, with the Scopes trial pitting the teaching of creationism or human evolution (American Civil Liberties Union, 2010) or how, in 2023, Governor Ron DeSantis of Florida used his political influence to limit what part of history could be included in the first Advanced Placement course in African American studies for the nation's high school students. However, as Ellen Condliffe Lagemann noted some time ago:

> One cannot understand the history of education [and the teaching profession] in the United States during the twentieth century unless one realises that Edward Thorndike won and John Dewey lost.
>
> (Lagemann, 1989, p. 184)

Indeed, the history of the teaching profession in America has been stormy and convoluted – and often framed by the struggle to determine who teaches what and how, and under what conditions they do so and at what cost. Over 200 years ago, America's teachers were hired to transmit values and, to some extent, the basic skills of the day. In the years since teachers have seen their salaries and working conditions improve and are better educated than ever. However, currently (as we write), in the third decade of the 21st century, the inner workings of a teacher's job have not changed much. Indeed, instead of chalkboards, one finds smartboards in the classroom. However, teaching in America retains vestiges of its past as "social housekeeping", where teachers were seen as those who can nurture students but need to take direction from administrative authorities.

Granted, teachers' wages and working conditions are far better today than yesterday. However, the occupational history of teaching includes long-standing control by laypeople, a lack of clarity and rigour in becoming a teacher, and limited prestige and income, restricting the professional possibilities of its members. As a result, teachers have struggled to stave off administrative and political demands to teach as they are told. At the same time, policymakers typically fill classrooms with underprepared teachers during shortages. The standing of teaching in American society has been complicated because teaching is a very public actAs historian David Labaree (2010, p. 180) noted, teachers are "way too familiar and too visible, and what they know seems to be all too common". Debates have raged over whether teachers should be formally prepared like other professions in university settings and then licensed, whether teachers should be unionised, and whether they are paid based on test scores. In *The Teacher Wars*, Dana Goldstein (2014) chronicles a range of reforms to fix America's teaching profession that have been tried in the past without producing widespread change.

Americans' view of teachers is complicated, and evidence points to the love–hate affair that a nation can have in an occupational group. Drawing on a range of time-series data from the 1970s to the early 2020s, Matt Kraft and Melissa Lyons (2022) point to the rise and fall of the teaching profession as defined by prestige, interest, preparation, and satisfaction. Of note is that over the last two decades, teachers reporting control over teaching (e.g. techniques, discipline, grading, and more) have dropped precipitously, and between 2018 and 2022, the percentage of parents who say they would like their children to be teachers dropped from an already low 46% to 37%.

Today, American society has a mixed view about teaching as an occupation. Gary Sykes (1983, p. 24) said: "Our social history reveals attitudes persistently equivocal towards teachers and a set of decidedly mixed messages about the status and value of this occupation". The same seems true today, exacerbated by the complications arising from the disruptions induced by COVID-19 in public schools and the rapid shift teachers had to make to "emergency" teaching. Researchers have found that teaching during and in the aftermath of the pandemic led to a significant drop in teachers' "sense of success". Now teacher stress is running at twice the rate of the general working public. In early 2023, teacher shortages were growing. More state legislatures were passing laws to restrict what teachers can teach, and the movement supporting private school tuition with public funds was gaining momentum, threatening the availability of resources teachers say are so important to serving every child. As Kraft and Lyons (2022, p.37) point out, the nation's policy leaders "must grapple with the rapid rise in deadly school shootings that undermine the basic sense of security (for teachers) necessary for effective teaching and learning".

In this historical context, American schools and their teachers, as Labaree (2010) suggests, are in a constant state of reform – albeit they often unintentionally generate new problems, which demand another set of reforms to address the previous ill-fated ones. It is not that America is devoid of successful educational reforms. David Cohen and Jal Mehta (2017) have pointed to successful ones (mass use of Advanced Placement courses) and their associated characteristics. Successful reforms meet the felt needs of the people who would implement them, offer solutions illuminating a real problem that educators had not been aware of, and take advantage of political, economic, or social circumstances.

However, the structure and culture of schooling in America most often position teachers as the targets of reform (or improvement), not the leaders of it. Anchored in the operating principles of scientific management, teachers work for principals who work for superintendents. In addition, most conceptions of scaling innovation in education rest on replicating or adopting some program – not their adaptation and reinvention by those who implement them. The latter is requisite for addressing the complexity of "digital age" schooling, now and in the future.

What can we take from this exposé of education in Australia, England, and the United States?

The central message is that the business of the teacher profession is under fire. While structural educational elements are called into question, realigned, designed, and reoriented, at the heart of each government decision is a realisation that the teaching profession is not up to scratch. To fully appreciate this significance is to realise that this does not, and would not, occur in the medical profession, nor for that matter nursing, even though they are concerned with the human condition.

While health funding is a constant government quibble, the professionalism of doctors and nurses is not questioned and, more pointedly, neither is their preparation regime. Although the teaching profession can push back on such reviews and reports, and it does, the reality is that all this must be treated as a wake-up call for action. Not by calling for more of the same and not by requesting more money, but by engaging in a fundamental rethink of what the teacher does, how they do it and where, but also how those who teach can position themselves to influence government and where their agency holds weight and rigour.

The teaching transformation agenda that is forming

- Socio-technological changes prompt governments to reassess the efficacy of education systems.
- Reports emphasise the necessity for reform in teaching quality, school performance, and curriculum relevance.
- Structural reforms such as centralising curriculum development and teaching regulation are imperative.

References

American Civil Liberties Union. (2010). *ACLU history: The Scopes 'Monkey Trial'.* www.aclu.org/other/aclu-history-scopes-monkey-trial

Australian Curriculum Assessment and Reporting Authority (ACARA). (2008). *The Australian Curriculum.* https://v9.australiancurriculum.edu.au/

Australian Government Department of Education. (2014). *Teacher Education Ministerial Advisory Group review.* www.education.gov.au/teaching-and-school-leadership/teacher-education-ministerial-advisory-group

Australian Government Department of Education. (2023). *Teacher Education Expert Panel.* www.education.gov.au/quality-initial-teacher-education-review/teacher-education-expert-panel

Australian Institute for Teaching and School Leadership (AITSL). (2005). *National professional standards for teachers.* www.aitsl.edu.au/teach/standards

Barr, A. (2008). *Melbourne Declaration on Educational Goals for Young Australians.* https://files.eric.ed.gov/fulltext/ED534449.pdf

Callahan, R. E. (1962). *Education and the cult of efficiency.* University of Chicago Press.

Cohen, D., & Mehta, J. (2017). Why reform sometimes succeeds: Understanding the conditions that produce reforms that last. *American Educational Research Journal, 54,* 644–690. https://doi.org/10.3102/0002831217700078

Darling-Hammond, L. (2022). *Possible futures: The policy changes we need to get there.* https://kappanonline.org/possible-futures-policy-changes-darling-hammond/

Federal Register of Legislation. (1973). *Schools Commission Act.* www.legislation.gov.au/C2004A00045/asmade/text

Goldstein, D. (2014). *The teacher wars.* Doubleday.

Gonski, D. (2011). *Review of funding for schooling: Final report.* https://apo.org.au/node/28263

House of Representative Committees. (1981). *Teacher Education Review*. www.aph.gov.
au/parliamentary_business/committees/house_of_representatives_committees?url=evt/
teachereduc/report/appendixd.htm

Kraft, M., & Lyons, M. (2022). *The rise and fall of the teaching profession: Prestige, interest,
preparation, and satisfaction over the last half century*. https://edworkingpapers.com/
index.php/ai22-679

Labaree, D. A. (2010). *Someone has to fail: The zero-sum game of public schooling*. Harvard
University Press. https://doi.org/10.2307/j.ctvjk2wpb.

Lagemann, E. C. (1989). The plural worlds of educational research. *History of Education
Quarterly*, 29(2), 185–214. https://doi.org/10.2307/368309

Linford, N. (2015). *Schools 'requiring improvement' face academisation*. https://school
sweek.co.uk/schools-requiring-improvement-face-academisation/

National Center for Education Statistics. (2023). Public school expenditures. Condition of
Education. U.S. Department of Education, Institute of Education Sciences. https://
nces.ed.gov/programs/coe/indicator/cmb

National Education Union. (2023). *Pay and Funding Campaign* . https://neu.org.uk/
campaigns/pay-and-funding-campaign

Ofsted. (2023). *Inspecting schools: Guide for maintained and academy schools*. www.gov.uk/
guidance/inspecting-schools-guide-for-maintained-and-academy-schools

Organisation for Economic Co-operation and Development (OECD). (2023). *Programme
for International Student Assessment*. www.oecd.org/pisa/

Parliament of Australia. (2003). *Ministerial Council on Education, Employment, Training
and Youth Affairs Taskforce on Teacher Quality*. www.aph.gov.au/DocumentStore.ashx?
id=712ad98a-d0f3-4dc0-93fa-c4e89b66aecc

The Guardian. (2023, February 7). *The Guardian view on arts education: A creativity crisis*.
www.theguardian.com/commentisfree/2023/feb/07/the-guardian-view-on-arts-educa
tion-a-creativity-crisis

Tyack, D., & Cuban, L. (1995). *Tinkering toward utopia: A century of public school reform*.
Harvard Education Press. www.gse.harvard.edu/ideas/ed-magazine/04/03/tinker
ing-toward-utopia-century-public-school-reform

UK Public General Acts. (1988). *Education Reform Act 1988*. www.legislation.gov.uk/ukp
ga/1988/40/contents

United Kingdom Department for Education. (2015). *2010 to 2015 government policy:
Academies and free schools*. www.gov.uk/government/publications/2010-to-2015-go
vernment-policy-academies-and-free-schools/2010-to-2015-government-policy-academ
ies-and-free-schools

4 What does it mean to be "educated"?

What's our key message?
- Socio-technological change defines the emergence of the Knowledge Society, leading to a "polycrisis" intersection of biopolitical, geopolitical, and geo-economic scenarios.
- Schools must adapt to prepare students for this radically different context, with teachers playing a pivotal role in reshaping education.
- Determining what it means to be educated involves grappling with societal purpose, philosophical positions, and the impact of irreversible social and cultural changes.
- Challenges such as youth mental health issues, technological mediation of social relations, and a politicised education environment further complicate the quest to redefine education for the future.

In our discussions to this point, we have revealed a societal circumstance characterised by ongoing socio-technological change, the emergence of the Knowledge Society, that radically redefines work and home life. English historian and Columbia University professor Adam Tooze (2023) describes it as an intersection of many biopolitical, geopolitical, and geo-economic crisis scenarios in the form of a "polycrisis". This engenders a picture of humanity muddling through in response to multiple intersecting crises in which "the whole is even more dangerous than the sum of the parts" (Lowrey, 2022). We have argued up to this point in the book that because schools prepare young people for work and life in such a context and given that the context is radically different from when schools were established, they must change accordingly. We further argued that the teacher and their teaching characteristics are pivotal in this reckoning. We have also questioned the amount of agency teachers currently have in their work, especially concerning contributing to a complex and disruptive agenda that is the prevailing systems of education. But as we argue in Chapter 11, this means a necessary change in what we prepare teachers for and how we do it. Before we can deal with such an agenda, we first need to discuss what the school and, more pointedly, the teacher

DOI: 10.4324/9781003303312-5

are to focus on. Put simply, we can debate and argue the structural and conceptual elements of a transformation of education, schooling, and teaching level, but we first need to decide what it should aim to achieve. This consideration is an essential task because any call for the transformation of teaching is mute until the focus of such a transformation is articulated. This defining, we contend, is not an easy task because the contemporary context of rapid social change and uncertainty impacts potential answers to the question, "What does it mean to be educated?"

What being educated means

Before we answer such a question, we first comment about the purpose of education because, in a constantly changing world, seeking clarity on purpose helps one cope with the ambiguity now present. When the question of what education should contribute to the young is posed, numerous possible answers emerge. Various positional patterns have occurred throughout the ages and have been written about *ad nauseam*. Some prioritise the qualities of the society where the young will live and contribute. Others are the individual's aspirations that can be achieved through high academic performance and establishing networks with the right people – the phenomena of "the old school tie". Some elevate individual human development over pragmatic demands such as job readiness. In many parts of Asia, education was learning to be human, emphasising character building where the family, community, and the world were prioritised. According to Confucius, the moral virtues of humanity or humanness (*jen*) and righteousness (*yi*) characterised a true gentleman or a superior man (Ng, 2009).

Still other aspirational ideas are located in the ideologically based issues and problems of traditional education. They include educational equality and justice, the justification of standardised curricula, testing, curriculum decisions, data-based decision-making, and the ethics of specific government funding arrangements. Accordingly, everyone involved in a Western education system holds, explicitly or implicitly, one or more philosophical positions or approaches about what is important. This includes such things as care for students, what makes students knowledgeable, the fostering of curiosity or rationality, autonomy, the enhancement of understanding, capturing the imagination, the socialising of students, accounting for individual different interests, abilities, and affinities for learning, and the development of associated dispositions and attitudes. For some, the school curriculum is criticised for being an instrument of control or social engineering to further the socio-political interests and goals of social groups defined as either oppressed or hegemonic. Depending on one's stance on one or combinations of these positions, what it means to be educated and what constitutes school improvement can appear to be a rabbit or a duck.

Determining the "best" education approach then is inextricably intertwined with further questions about ethics, metaphysics, and epistemology, the stuff of philosophy. Moral considerations, for example, are already embedded in ideas such as "equal access", "inclusion", "diversity", "preparation for jobs", "the kind of society and environment we want to create", becoming an "informed citizen", and "social justice". There is no neutral knowledge regarding how to interpret society and history and the role of education in it. Moreover, there is no independent evaluative viewpoint from which one tradition can be judged superior to another, as much as there is no standard of rationality independent of some philosophical tradition. However, psychological and anthropological evidence is that human societies espouse a small number of core moral values. They include benevolence, fairness, loyalty, respect for authority, personal purity in body and mind, and freedom from oppressive control by others. Perhaps education policy should embed these as generic values.

In short, there are differences, incompatibilities, and agreements in different philosophical traditions that education policy and practice tend to quickly bypass to implement political decisions about what it means to be educated. If one seeks to answer our focal question, influencing a government policy position is crucial when the intended outcome is a change in the school curriculum. Put another way, different viewpoints suggest that there is no defensible position about whether an education practice or policy is morally "right". As Campbell (2019, p. 47) puts it, "moral disagreements resist resolution, however intelligent, informed, and respectful the disputants may be because moral knowledge is impossible". This is not to deny others their moral positions on the purposes of education. Instead, it is an admission that we, as authors, do not believe this book is the place to engage in a 2,000-year-old debate where the outcome is indeterminate *a priori*. The criteria determining the principles for what an "education" means is a matter of political power, which brings us to the times in which we are living and the role that governments, as society's authority, have to play in resolving. However, we identify two interrelated circumstances that offer criteria for clarifying the purposes of education and thus contribute to our answering to the question of what it means to be educated. They are irreversible social-cultural changes shaping a new era and, by direct association, the impact this is having on the wellbeing of people – especially the young – and their capacities to deal with a world that is as confusing to them as it is muddling to their parents.

Irreversible social, cultural, and behavioural changes shape a "change of era"

New ideas, trends, approaches, and social behaviours that spread across schools, jurisdictions, and systems like wildfire impact education. In short, it is a "tipping point" period when irreversible social, cultural, and behavioural changes have and continue to shape the present and future. To illustrate such changes, futurists like Eric Jensen (2011) argue that information and intelligence have become the domain of computers, and societies place more value on human abilities that cannot be automated: emotion, imagination, myth, and ritual. Industrial-age ideas like quality, efficiency, and reliability no longer have appeal. The life of the information economy that began in the early 1950s is predicted to be about 75 to 80 years, ending somewhere in the late 2020s. At this point, it is predicted that the next life cycle curve in a biotechnology era will take off, each with a plethora of "the new" that impacts the lives of everyone on the planet. This can only lead to more radical societal disruptions, further disorganising the "what it means to be educated" conundrum.

Historically, era changes have seen the shift in power from the church and family to government and increasingly to the power of social media tribes. In today's world, the shift towards a focus on talent and human capital online is overwhelming, where everything is connected to everything and everybody to everybody, in what Stan Davis (2001), a widely recognised visionary, calls "from crunching to connecting". He points out that a characteristic of this shift is that the control of personal resources has shifted from institutions to individuals: we have all noticed in our personal banking, health, and workplaces, dealings with corporations, government, our human resource departments and businesses that we now do the work. In schooling, as homeschooling illustrated during the COVID-19 pandemic, proximity and distance between the teacher and the student are not the issue as much as the connectivity between the spaces and how that space is used. One can assume that students in online environments, among many other changes, will need to take on more responsibility in selecting and executing online programs than in physical classroom settings. Nevertheless, this also prefigures the new work and focus of those who teach and the role and function of what is meant by "a school".

In the teaching profession, an unrelenting pressure on teaching is the switch between what is being taught and what students are learning and their ownership and passion for it. The language of emotion impacts everything from education policy decisions to how teachers, school leaders, lecturers, and even vice-chancellors work with others. Virtue is prized and monetarised above traditional academic and scholarly values, and organisations thrive based on their stories and myths, irrespective of their truth values. In many instances of this shift, education appears susceptible to devaluing its prime knowledge products in favour of its story virtuosity. Unsurprisingly, teachers and school leaders feel the heat of a "toxic" workplace as they attempt to resolve contradictions between the management structures, organisational culture, and the surge of new social and cultural demands on them.

A decisive outcome of the change from an industrial era is the heightened awareness of social inequalities, global environmental degradation, pollution, and climate change, which younger generations aspire to correct. With its economy heavily reliant on information, the Knowledge Society has been radically democratising globally, but its unresolved Achilles' heel is privacy and control by private interests. The most significant predicted problems of the future bioeconomy are bound to be ethical dilemmas involving the human genome and life. Important intellectual and practical issues such as these imply that citizens should have the knowledge, skills, and judgement capacities to understand and take a position on what is at stake. The *prima facie* case for the universal service that schools provide on behalf of societies and to the benefit of individuals is that "schooling", and its associated post-school pathways, is the logical place to start irrespective of the form it might take.

With that proposition in mind, we take the stance that it is too early to give up on education as an instrument of social change. Schools have a place in our modern society, albeit with a rethought logic, new positionings, and new roles in order to have an effect within society. However, as later chapters outline, doing what schools have done for a century or devising new education policies and processes using mindsets that hark back to an era now long gone are unlikely to be adequate as the basis for being educated in the years to come. In a later chapter, we will argue that the "local school", with its traditional logic and structures, as generations have known it, is already obsolete, requiring a plan to identify and mitigate risk for teaching, staffing, teacher education, and resources. This needs to happen before it becomes a crisis. We further argue that what it means to be educated is being held hostage by the traditions of how our schools are organised and staffed. The enormity of the changes needed is mind-bending and, therefore, best put to one side of the halls of politics.

To add further complexity, as we write, a quick survey of the online news media indicates a pressing list of challenges: climate change defined as an "emergency", inflation, the continuing COVID-19 pandemic, public health service delivery failures, energy emergencies, the threat of global war, the reckonings of racial justice, the social media culture of shaming and suppressing opinion by "cancelling" people and ideas that are the shaping the history of our times. Schools are dealing with the effects of a change of era manifesting in social and psychological stress in young people. Teacher education continues to be defensive as its delivery models are increasingly irrelevant in the face of schools becoming community hubs. The efficacy and status of university-based teacher education have become major political concerns for governments. In England, significant changes have occurred in teacher education, which has been less about improving its relevance and more about a political strategy to marginalise universities by enabling other providers to enter the teacher education field. As advances in the science of learning have become more central in systems of whole-child education, universities seemingly have become less relevant in preparing teachers for it. Our point is that education, teaching, and schools are enmeshed in a highly politicised environment and attempting to change it from within is highly problematic.

The young and their wellbeing

There is acute public alarm about youth suicide rates, despair leading to opioid overdoses, and decreasing overall life expectancy. Many American school-aged children do not feel that they belong in their school. People of colour and immigrants, in particular, sense that they are not accepted or seen as equals. Teen disengagement in American schools is rising. In England, the education journey has been reported to be a huge stress for young people, leading to a general rise in mental health problems, including self-harming. Educators are particularly interested in the alienation of the young during the pandemic and the pressures the education system applies to them. Social distancing measures, physical isolation during COVID-19 lockdowns, sudden loss of social interaction, and the stress of moving to remote schooling have had an impact on the mental health of many Australian children. This is seen in increased days absent from school and lower average NAPLAN test scores for students with mental disorders compared to those without them. At every turn, the media reminds the young that they will never own a house to live in, that jobs are disappearing, the world is likely to end soon from the climate emergency, and that the opportunities historically presented to their parents' generation are remote for them.

The "Eliza effect" – the unconscious acceptance that computer behaviour is analogous to human behaviour – means that when a device appears "smart" and clever, humans interacting with it will believe it is. Younger generations are tied to a world in which technology mediates social relations. Social media accounts can be diverted or blocked, and friends can be immediately "unfriended". According to Turkle (2011), this environment encourages a type of narcissism when others are thought of as a problem to be managed or a resource to be exploited. For commentators and educators, there is a crisis that schools are *ipso facto* expected to resolve. There are serious embedded problems here for society, but whether they are "educational" rather than political or cultural is another matter. Following the COVID-19 impact on schooling, there are reports that Kindergarten to 12 teachers are more likely than other government employees to say they have had difficulty adjusting to changes brought on by the pandemic. Higher levels of anxiety, stress, and burnout are reported across Australia, the United States, and England among teachers. This is because, in addition to dealing with impacts at the personal level, they are also dealing with changed work practices and with new participants in the process of learning, including parents who are now seemingly more informed due to homeschooling experiences. These factors are purely symptomatic because the experience of the pandemic misjudges the underlying causes of disruption affecting teachers, namely epoch change. They are in an uncomfortable situation that places them between the past idea of a "school" and the emerging realities of an unknown and potentially uncontrolled future. Anxiety, stress, and burnout are all symptoms of people in such liminal spaces.

In times of increased anxiety – like the one in which we find ourselves – questions of personal and collective identity inevitably arise. In a democracy, layers of identity and connections with people with whom we may share little in common in other ways are the basis for civic life and participation. The state's legitimacy and ability to govern turn on identification with the commonalities between disparate people, so the decline of trust and lack of national identity is an obvious danger to a "way of life". It is reported that compromise on political issues is difficult in England because of distrust of the "other side", and an increasing number of issues get tied up in a sense of identity. Australian public discourse and political behaviour are marked by personal attacks, wild exaggeration and the endless repeating of slogans. Questionable understanding and dwindling commitment to democratic social arrangements by statist and market liberals in the professional-managerial class fill even fashion magazines. Author Christopher Lasch (2010) questions whether members of the new globally oriented US elite think of themselves as American. Despite the apparent divisions involving "identity", identity and its associated concepts and practices have become indispensable in contemporary education policy and procedural discourse. Nonetheless, it has complex and unresolved implications for models of the self, political inclusiveness, social solidarity, and resistance possibilities. It is already clear, author Christina Heyes (2002) maintains, that the use of the controversial term "identity" raises a host of philosophical questions that we suggest ought to be made transparent and, in some credible fashion, resolved before the wholesale, glib imposition of "identity politics" ontology is universally applied by teacher education schools, government and independent school authorities, and politicians.

We borrow Sacasas' (2013) term "Borg Complex" to illustrate how social justice theory in education and society is aptly summed up by the phrase, "Resistance is futile". It fosters foreclosure on the possibility of contrary thinking about and taking responsibility for education goals and operations, including the preparation of teachers. It is particularly pernicious for liberal democratic principles, as Table 4.1 illustrates.

The "fix it at school" solution to social problems looks simple to experts and bureaucrats who recycle and adapt pre-existing solutions to new or emerging problems, regardless of the policy problem originating in these societies' social and cultural fabric. Add in a tendency for schools to go with the latest "education fads" and to realise later that the investment did not pan out only confirms it all as a complex problem to deal with. Determining what it means to be educated in such a world requires a break from a system of school education infamous for its long tail of underachievement, and a lack of professional leadership provides an apparent reason not to continue that course of action. Viewed through the prism of a "polycrisis", the shocks in education across the West are not exogenous disruptions and unpredictable "events" but the result of causal chains that stretch back to the 1950s. A change of purpose, design, and performance is needed to move from a surplus of similar programs, employing similar people with similar educational backgrounds, working in similar jobs, coming up with similar ideas, and producing similar outcomes at similar costs and quality. There is a *prima facie* case that too much is thrust on schools, and their role might be enhanced by

Table 4.1 Borg Complex indicators: resistance is assumed to be heretical and immoral.

Makes grandiose but unsupported claims for the superiority of social justice education concepts.
Uses the term *Luddite* or "Old School" a-historically and as a casual slur.
Dismisses genuine concerns.
Equates resistance or caution to reactionary nostalgia.
Starkly and matter-of-factly frames the case for overcoming liberal curriculum, teaching, and governance models.
Announces a bleak future for those who refuse to assimilate.
Expresses contemptuous disregard for past cultural achievements.
Refers to historical antecedents solely to dismiss present concerns.

reducing the scope of their activities to a specialised, quality "teaching" institution, understood broadly. The problem is that if education can compensate (a bit) for social disruptions, one needs to know what to do and ensure that governance, schools, and teachers working with allied professionals can do it together – not in their organisational siloes.

So, what does it mean to be educated?

What it means to be educated today and into the future is prefigured by the certainty that education is lifelong and is charged with preparing people for change and uncertainty. While we chiefly concern ourselves in this book with compulsory schooling, the reality is that being educated is a lifelong journey. This implicates technical colleges, universities, private tutors, and the professional learning and training entities that abound either in-house or as part of a new education market. The underpinning assumption in all this, however, is that being educated implies personal competency in what can be called "21st-century skills" – so that has all people have equitable access to opportunity and life chances but are armed with strategies to maintain their sense of wellbeing. We explore these ideas further in Chapter 5. We make the point here that schooling must transform quickly to a point where acquiring basic literacy and numeracy skills is no longer the "big issue" of schooling in government reports. Acquiring them should be a given and a teaching competency that all teachers have honed.

Being educated also assumes that the educated have substantive knowledge that enables and authorises them to think critically, have broad perspectives, be discerning and creative, and have a rich understanding of themselves, their society and cultures, and their place in the world. Not to mention knowing key things and being able to do specific things confidently. In keeping with that principle and its implementation, specific ideologies, opinions, or perspectives of authors and speakers ought not to restrict the diversity of opinion on education content and practice, subject to the usual caveats around obscenity, child pornography, inciting violence, and defamation, including libel and slander. Coming to a position on what it means to be educated is to appreciate that education is about young people learning things to a competent level that positions them for a productive and meaningful life.

All of this needs to be pinned down through a national conversation about what it means to be educated, and this implicates governments who should lead and inspire and accordingly define the type of society they want for their populace. In many ways, this can be understood as a vision for one's nation but also a redefining of what success is and how success is nurtured through education. The point here is that being educated is for and about modern society, and accordingly, the specifics about what is "in" and what is "out" of the mandated curriculum is a matter for the government to decide when policies are developed. We say this to counter the many conflicting perspectives and to outline how important things such as "education" should be resolved in democracies. Accordingly, we suggest that this national narrative includes a mature debate where new success criteria are prefigured to capture the many opportunities, potentials, and talent aspirations that feed and motivate people in a Knowledge Society. These new success criteria will seek to challenge and mature assumptions that success at school is just a university entrance score, a school captain's badge, or membership of the "in-crowd": legacies that our current system of schooling tends to champion and which causes it to get caught up in tinkering and lamenting the past. More fundamentally, school education is about young people acquiring essential knowledge as foundations for lifelong learning scenarios. We have signalled the idea of new success criteria as the starting point for resolving the conflicts that currently plague curriculum offerings. Being educated, therefore, embodies society's aspirational vision for its people. In Chapter 5, we outline what these curriculum resolutions should focus on.

The teaching transformation agenda that is forming

- Recognising the societal shift towards a Knowledge Society and implementing modification to the pre-existing model of schooling through ongoing socio-technological change.
- Redesigning the school curriculum to focus on core knowledge and skills that resonate with a society built on dealing with generating and exploiting knowledge for various gains.
- Acknowledging the pivotal role of teachers in preparing students for work and life in a rapidly changing context.
- Advocating for a transformation of education to focus on lifelong learning, critical thinking, broad perspectives, and meaningful engagement with society and culture.

References

Campbell, C. S. (2019). The unbearable burden of suffering: Moral crisis or structural failure? *The American Journal of Bioethics*, 19(10), 46–47. https://doi.org/10.1080/15265161.2019.1653399

Heyes, C. (2002). Identity politics. In E. N. Zalta (Ed.), *Stanford encyclopedia of philosophy archive*. https://plato.sydney.edu.au/archives/fall2017/entries/identity-politics/

Jensen, E. (2011). *Arts with the brain in mind*. Association for Supervision and Curriculum Development. www.daneshnamehicsa.ir/userfiles/files/1/13-%20Arts%20with%20the%20brain%20in%20mind%20(2001,%20ASCD).pdf

Lasch, C. (2010). *The revolt of the elites and the betrayal of democracy*. W. W. Norton & Company.

Lowrey, A. (2022, July 5). A crisis historian has some bad news for us. *The Atlantic*. www.theatlantic.com/ideas/archive/2022/07/adam-tooze-chartbook-substack-newsletter-inflation-crisis/661467/

Ng, R. M.-C. (2009). College and character: What did Confucius teach us about the importance of integrating ethics, character, learning, and education? *Journal of College and Character*, 10(4). https://doi.org/10.2202/1940-1639.1045

Sacasas, L. M. (2013). *Borg Complex: A primer.* https://thefrailestthing.com/2013/03/01/borg-complex-a-primer/

Tooze, A. (2023). *Adam Tooze: Kathryn and Shelby Cullom Davis Professor of History.* https://history.columbia.edu/person/adam-tooze/

Turkle, S. (2011). *Alone together: Why we expect more from technology and less from each other.* Basic Books.

Ubiquity. (2001). *A few ideas from Stan Davis.* https://ubiquity.acm.org/article.cfm?id=380745

Part 2

Prefiguring changes to teaching, schooling, and teacher education

5   A rethink of the school curriculum

What's our key message?

- Education should be viewed as a lifelong process aimed at preparing individuals for constant change and uncertainty.
- The competitive advantage in the modern business world lies in the ability of businesses to learn, pivot, and respond to markets rapidly – this should be taught in schools.
- A rethink of the school curriculum is necessary to address issues such as wellbeing, the balance between old and new knowledge, and education's role within society.
- The COVID-19 pandemic has highlighted the potential for technology to revolutionise education, prompting a reconsideration of traditional schooling models.

In Chapter 4, we argued that "being educated" is prefigured by the certainty that education must be a lifelong process designed to prepare people for change and uncertainty. It also means people know about and can do critical things. A dynamic and rapidly changing environment means that in the business world, for example, "knowing" is no longer sufficient – how quickly a business can learn, pivot, and respond to markets is now the competitive advantage. In the same way, education and schooling will need people with the same mindset. Our argument also assumes that there is a substantive, specific knowledge base that enables and authorises people to think critically, deal with ambiguity, be discerning and creative, and have a rich understanding of themselves, society, and their place in the world. Accordingly, new success criteria are prefigured to capture the many opportunities, potentials, and talent aspirations that feed and motivate people in a Knowledge Society. Again, we make the point that the knowledge base is dynamic, given how quickly information is generated in current times and the lifelong learning process. There is tension though when new technologies, emerging research, and issues specific to the local context and deeply held cultural traditions demand a move from thinking that knowledge is static – that there is one

DOI: 10.4324/9781003303312-7

truth, and civilisation will not progress. Our discussion now explores the hallmarks of a rethink of the school curriculum. In effect, we take the central issues from Chapter 4 and locate them in the context of a school curriculum response. Thus, we identify three themes that guide a discussion about how to deal with the current contested and overcrowded curriculum and reposition it for the future. Putting aside the mandate of "the basics" (reading and writing) because they are a given in any curriculum, the three themes are (i) wellbeing as the centrepiece of curriculum aspirations, (ii) the premise of old and new knowledge, and (iii) education and its interplay within and for society.

Wellbeing as the centrepiece of curriculum aspirations

Considering the context of ongoing social change, it is fair to suggest that growing up is complex and challenging today. It is complex because technology is pervasive, disruptive, and challenging, and keeping up to date and connected means living in a constant state of flux. While every generation has lamented the ravine that is the transition from childhood into adulthood, in the modern world constant change, with the anxieties that emerge from the unknown and apparent pending catastrophes, is creating issues around wellbeing. Wellbeing is related to the individual's capacity to understand, cope with, and ultimately thrive in a world of constant change, ambiguity, uncertainty, and contradiction. This demands ensuring it is a crucial curriculum consideration today and into the future. In education, wellbeing for students is evident when they feel confident and function so that their physical, social, and emotional life experience enables learning, ensures resilience, and readies them for the demands of a Knowledge Society. This seemingly sound proposition is reflected in a growing concern many in society have about declining states of mental health and lack of resilience in young people and the growing calls for schools and teachers to respond.

Wellness as a curriculum centrepiece demands a comparison of life circumstances with social norms and values, not just in the student's milieu but globally. For an individual, wellbeing is not a fixed state. It can change from day to day, month to month, and year to year, a factor important in education as students face success and failure in their studies and their extra-curricular activities. The good news is that ensuring students feel good and function well results in their physical, social, mental, and emotional life experiences fostering learning. Adjustment is the condition of a person who can adapt to physical, work, and social changes. It refers to balancing conflicting needs or needs challenged by environmental obstacles and working toward a solution. It is a professional undertaking for which teachers and school leaders have responsibility. It is a pedagogical responsibility. This is not a new issue; as author Alf Lundgren (1982, p. 36) insisted 40 years ago, significant pressures on students and teachers "are determined outside the teaching process" and hence "outside the control of teachers and students", but how the school deals with them in the day-to-day practices of teaching and organisation are where the interests of educators have to be directed as it is fundamental to student wellbeing. This notion of wellbeing must be understood from two broad standpoints. The first is "care", and the second is "mastery".

Care and wellbeing

Living in a highly changing world, with increased financial pressures and demands of consumerism on families, this means parents and caregivers are inclined to prioritise employment – their work. This is evidenced by the booming daycare business and before/after/vacation school care, now familiar features for many children in developed economies. The 9 am to 3 pm nature of schooling is no longer the limit of care necessary, and the shift from parental care to that provided by others also has implications for a child's development and wellbeing. We do not advocate extending the teacher's role to be more responsible for a child's care over a longer day. We argue that playground supervision, traffic control duties before and after school, and a range of administrative tasks related to school management should not be in the scope of professional pedagogical experts. We discuss the case in more detail in later chapters. Suffice it to say that pilots do not fuel aircraft, and cardiologists do not clean offices. They fly passengers safely and save lives through highly specialist interventions, respectively, and according to the codified knowledge and skill for which they are qualified.

The point is that adding hours to the day for care or "wellbeing" courses is not the solution in an already crowded curriculum. Suppose the increasing prevalence of wellbeing interventions in society is necessary. In that case, we argue they are the purview of other professionals and potentially new roles required in a reconfigured approach to schooling. Our point here is that the wellbeing of young people is an issue in modern society and that the education system needs to consider it and design for it accordingly. In a later chapter, we introduce the concept of a multi-disciplinary schooling workforce, which elaborates on these contentions.

Wellbeing and mastery

While various authors discuss, examine, and try to predict the future, we have no precise data or insight about it. At best, we can determine trends in data and attempt to extrapolate this to inform possible outcomes. Given the increasing uncertainty in our society and economy, longer-term projects often become unreliable. Our position then is that our task is to think about and recognise what we call "loose bricks" and "weak signals", the signs of change that will inevitably affect education, and how the institutions of education might lead, adapt, or collapse as an effect. Rather than rejecting the past as the cause of dystopian society on Orwellian proportions, we insist that the curriculum, more than ever, should equip students to comprehend the past and present so that they can explore the possibility of future events and trends based on knowledge rather than personal attitudes and feelings. We seek systematic alternatives rather than a cacophony of personal views regarding what education means.

The core issue here is to assist students in mastering increasingly complex cognitive tasks, skills, and abilities that enable them to comprehend and have some agency to deal with constant change, ambiguity, uncertainty, and contradiction, as well as rewards and a happy life. Knowledge, understanding, and a game plan in tandem are the antidotes that "education" can provide to counter the victimhood scourge that depowers even the most resilient of contemporary students and teachers. Without viable alternatives, it resides in the accumulated collections of disciplines across science, the arts, humanities, languages, literature, the trades, and technology. The products of human ingenuity are the property of each emergent generation, and the school is where the acculturation into such knowledge is expected. An objective that education – schooling, training, and higher education – must have in common. The deliberate development of such knowledge, skills, and abilities in all students is the contemporary task of education (Simon, 1994).

The premise of old and new knowledge

Education is an enormous industry undertaken at insatiable costs yet traditionally lags behind social and technological developments. Key Performance Indicators and standardised tests among a host of other order-maintaining management processes ensure that, as an institution, education is better adapted to the transmission of cultural heritage than it is to renew it. In today's fast-changing world, "cultural lag" – educating for a world that no longer exists – and resistance to change pose significant challenges to what should be taught and how it is presented. As we mentioned in early chapters and based on the published evidence, most parents who send their children to schools in England, the United States, and Australia, for example, want them to have the education they had and still have faith in. Education is the pathway through which ordinary folk can imagine a change in their circumstances as their children accumulate knowledge and learn to interpret and use it for access to jobs and a productive life. Parents still primarily value schools' academic performance and note school performance data published by education authorities where available when choosing a school.

Parents also assume their children will be safe and protected at school and be taught essential skills and knowledge for which the school is accountable. In their day, communication skills came from written and spoken communication across several years of practice. They gained problem-solving skills from solving problems in these classes, and higher-order cognitive skills came from studying "traditional" subjects such as English, geography, and mathematics. The consensus across Australia, the United States, and England among parents is remarkable: they believe in knowledge and the power of good teaching among a raft of additional features, some tempered by cultural and class differences. Their fondest school memories revolve around the "good teachers" who motivated and inspired them, advocating for skilled teaching and equal opportunities for every child. Conversely, they vehemently object when it does not happen, especially when favourable school reports fail to materialise. The irony is that in a survey reported by esteemed academic Professor John Hattie (2016), when asked about the major influences on school achievement and wellbeing, a survey of Australian parents paradoxically nominated the very things that have the most negligible effect on the learning lives of students. Hattie emphasises that high-performing systems tend to prioritise the quality of teaching and "it is not structural solutions but expertise that matters", which is a fundamental principle for policymakers, and "if we appease the parents and the voters, we destroy the optimal education for their children. We need a reboot in the narrative of schooling".

What is evident in all this is that being literate and numerate and knowing key things are still valued by society and fundamental to student engagement in the school curriculum. We do not see this logic as having to change. However, curriculum elements have wide currency because they are what workers who make up significant proportions of the US, English, and Australian workforces expect from education. Skilled workers also share the knowledge and skill set of such workers in what were previously "blue collar" industries as workplaces are digitised and automated. Emergent generational differences mark a definite shift in the appropriate knowledge product younger parents want for their children's education compared to other generations. Millennial parents in China, North America, the UK, and Spain, for example, prefer creative, flexible schools with a global outlook and concentrate on soft skills and personal attitudes rather than proficiency in academic subjects alone. They want their children to achieve outstanding academic results like Gen X'ers and Baby Boomers. However, now they want far more from their child's broader education: they want schools to enable students to be creative, innovative, resilient, and to have a sense of purpose that promotes emotional and mental wellbeing, language learning, and an entrepreneurial mentality. Further, they want children to have critical thinking capacity and an international outlook. The ability to manage conflict and to be adaptable for a future they cannot quite define yet, so their children are ready for life in an uncertain world, are highly prized. Without wishing to prescribe a laundry list, Table 5.1 indicates 21st-century knowledge, skills, and behavioural characteristics widely mentioned by parents and policy sources.

Generational similarities and differences undoubtedly occur within cohorts of teachers as well. While plenty of these characteristics and attributes have the ring of the new about them, they remain within the recognisable model of a school everywhere. Significantly, as noted, they rely on the past for their knowledge content to formulate alternatives and on pedagogical techniques to optimise learning. Moreover, without policy nuance about "pop futures", they draw our attention to the same comfortable education world that policymakers and, dare we say it, teacher educators and parents have in mind. Everything that appears to be preparation for future success instead narrows its chances of survival. There is now an active global market for such an education product, and we can anticipate a rash of policy mandates emphasising these valuable attributes.

Education and its interplay within and for society

Can education impact society, or does society overwhelm education's best efforts to achieve moral ends? Our view is that there is sufficient faith in the efficacy of education to provide individuals with the wherewithal for a rich life and society with the resources to guarantee equality, safety, and a productive life. We believe the central claim in education is that it has particular moral importance through

Table 5.1 Indicative definitions of 21st-century skills.

Literacy	Ability to read, understand, and use written language
Numeracy	Ability to use numbers and other symbols to understand and express quantitative relationships
Scientific Literacy	Ability to use best-available scientific knowledge and principles to understand one's environment, ask questions, and test hypotheses
ICT Literacy	Ability to use and create technology-based content, including finding and sharing information, answering questions, interacting with other people, and computer programming
Financial Literacy	Ability to understand and apply conceptual and numerical aspects of finance in practice
Cultural and Civic Literacy	Ability to understand, appreciate, analyse, and apply credible knowledge of the humanities across history/philosophy/the arts
Critical Thinking/Problem-Solving	Capacity to identify, analyse, and evaluate situations, ideas, and information to formulate responses and solutions in both scientific and cultural realms
Creativity	Ability to imagine and devise new, innovative ways of dealing with problems, answering questions, or expressing meaning through the application, synthesis, or repurposing of knowledge
Communication	Ability to listen to, understand, convey, and contextualise information through verbal, non-verbal, visual, and written means, including cross-culturally
Collaboration	Ability to work in a team towards a common goal, including the ability to prevent and manage conflict
Curiosity	Ability and desire to ask questions and to demonstrate open-mindedness and inquisitiveness
Initiative	Ability and desire to proactively undertake a new task or goal
Persistence/Grit	Ability to sustain interest and effort and to persevere to accomplish a task or goal
Adaptability	Ability to change plans, methods, opinions, or goals in light of new data, information, and theories
Leadership	Ability to effectively direct, guide, and inspire others to accomplish a common goal
Social and Cultural Awareness	Ability to comprehend the role of the other, interact with other people, and behave in a socially, culturally, and ethically appropriate way

what it makes possible, namely, attempts to negate the persistent historical failure to achieve full inclusion in power structures for members of marginalised groups. Under the cultural, social, and economic assumptions of the present about "inclusion" and "equity" that are overwhelmingly dominant in public discourse right now is a non-negotiable goal of education. The concept of inclusion and what it generically means and the fostering of a robust sense of self in students is clearly in the domain of schooling. Preparing teachers with the most effective teaching capacities and stocks of knowledge to deliver knowledge-rich learning experiences in appealing ways is of prime importance in teacher preparation and policy mandates.

Preparation for civic life and participation in a democracy has precise national and individual functions that form part of education's sphere of responsibility. Despite the persistent historical failure of liberal democracies to achieve full inclusion in power structures for members of marginalised groups, we maintain that understanding that everyone possesses layers of identity and multiple connections with people with whom they may share little in common in other ways is essential to any robust functional society. A critical function of schooling is reinforcing what people have in common due to the overlapping nature of social group memberships at the local and global level. This means their differences are less important, thus countering the division, parochialism, and irrationality that some claim to be characteristic of Western societies today. Further, the development of perspective about the past and contemporary web-based cultures that share generational mores via social and communications media are integral to realising one's position locally and as a member of humanity. Again, education probably has a central role in unpicking the inconsistencies of core Western achievements such as multi-culturalism made possible by liberal democratic states. There are tensions, such as defending the rights of minority cultures while prohibiting illegal cultural practices under state law. Rapprochements between "liberalism" and "identity politics" on these fundamental matters definitively impact what it means to be educated today. We maintain that there are other possibilities regarding the school's role in preparing for jobs, which irrevocably imply mathematics, physics, engineering, and ICT-related knowledge and skills for all. The promise of transdisciplinary suggests that these disciplines and the arts, humanities, and social sciences have roles to play in developing local and global sensitivities and respect for the school's product, educated graduates.

What we learnt from the COVID-19 pandemic

The home–school education adaptations developed during the global pandemic may well be noted as the turning point for the future of schools, and one might speculate also for teaching. Forced by lockdowns, governments, teachers, and schools needed to find ways to use technological resources such as the internet to assemble and deliver educational programs designed to teach students. Not all such programs were successful, and not all teachers and students had enjoyable experiences because neither students, teachers, nor parents were well prepared for what they faced. However, there is some evidence that online and hybrid programs were as effective as traditional face-to-face classes or demonstrated potential if factors such as connectivity and access were dealt with. It is apparent today that the former utopian goal of individualised instruction in classrooms based on each student's characteristics and education history could be achieved with "intelligent" devices and systematic programs constructed on credible cognitive science research.

Curiously, accomplishing the means to individualise radically is based on the means described as "mass customising", a term that hitherto had negative connotations. Contemporary IT, such as artificial intelligence, virtual reality, augmented reality, and the increasing sophistication of connectivity, reinforce Hattie's (2021) plea to make schooling a more inviting experience for learning for all possible. Nevertheless, there are seriously under-examined prerequisites concealed in much of the technological hype about future education. They include the architecture and functioning of human brains and the conditions for optimising learning identified in modern education, for example, Cognitive Load Theory (CLT). CLT has revealed conditions for the meaningful learning of complex cognitive tasks and has contributed to fields including school teaching and instructional design. The theory uses verified knowledge about universal human cognitive structures, with long-term memory being described as "the central structure of human cognition", albeit operating with individual variations (Paas et al., 2010, p. 116). One wonders how many teacher education schools include this work and how many teachers are sufficiently competent to create instructional designed programs and lessons in addition to learning how to use the devices that have the potential to be educative.

Imagine if students do not want to absorb school teaching passively because they are acculturated to gamified, contextual experiences from their immersion in media and the internet. Again, take seriously the reality that many younger-generation students already possess a digital persona that carries over into the metaverse from the real world. Further, education remains a significant mandated commitment by the young and throughout later life. In that case, participants will want "skin in the game" to validate how they choose – or are coerced by circumstances – to spend their time. Experience, identity, and ownership in education institutions may well be one of the practical keys to solving the present concerns with "care", life skills, and 21st-century skills as the realisation dawns that, in the metaverse, you are less a user than a member. Education could become a "cause" for humanity rather than an institution required by the state, or, in this high-stakes game, it could go the other way.

According to Hackl et al. (2022), the early signs are there for schools and universities worldwide that technologies offer promising possibilities. Engineers are creating the building blocks of the metaverse, and entrepreneurs, both within and beyond the education community, will have to figure out what to do with them. Amara's Law probably applies: we tend to overestimate the impact of new technology in the short run, but we underestimate it in the long run, despite the danger of ending up with "virtual reality with unskippable ads" or the market taking over the education experience. We do not propose closing schools and moving to online education provision. Schools are essential in socialising younger generations, supporting parental work commitments, and acting as community centres in many places. How they fit into digitised societies now and into the future with presumably different criteria for what it means to be educated is what we think now needs to be determined. However, the point is that these critical functions can be undertaken by alternative means, so schools can be released from attempting them in addition to their central "teaching" role. Nevertheless, all this needs to be managed for education effects, and this implicates a rethink of the role and function of the schoolteacher – a theme we explore in Chapter 7.

Our discussion in this chapter have told us that a new schooling curriculum needs to reflect society's future needs and, accordingly, a prefiguring of what young people need to know and be able to do in readiness for a world built on uncertainty, ambiguity, and change. We have argued that there is still a traditional knowledge base for young people to learn, such as literacy and numeracy. However, elements such as wellbeing and new knowledge presuppose a schooling experience that represents a refurbishment of the existing curriculum mandate and the operating logic for a "future school". From a reverse perspective, this prefigures the notion of new success criteria to capture the many opportunities, potentials, and talent aspirations that feed and motivate people in a Knowledge Society. This leads us to examine the new business of teaching and schooling in the following chapters.

The teaching transformation agenda that is forming

- Understanding that schools must adapt to prepare youth for ongoing socio-technological change and the emergence of the Knowledge Society.
- Understanding that educational transformation necessitates a clear understanding of the aims and objectives of society.
- Acknowledgement of the impact of technological advancements and connectivity on teaching and learning.
- Recognition of the role of education in preparing individuals for lifelong learning and navigating change and uncertainty.

References

Hackl, C., Lueth, D., Di Bartolo, T., Arkontaky, J., & Siu, Y. (2022). *Navigating the metaverse: A guide to limitless possibilities in a Web 3.0 world*. Wiley.

Hattie, J. (2016). *Shifting away from distractions to improve Australia's schools: Time for a reboot.* https://education.unimelb.edu.au/news-and-events/events/2016/dls/shifting-away-from-distractions-to-improve-australias-schools

Hattie, J. (2021). *An ode to expertise: What have we learnt from COVID and how can we apply our new learning?*www.educationtoday.com.au/news-detail/An-Ode-to-Expertise-5409

Lundgren, U. P. (1982). Between schooling and education: Notes on curriculum changes within the second generation of school reforms in Sweden. *Paper presented at the Annual Meeting of the American Educational Research Association, New York, March 19–23, 1982.* https://eric.ed.gov/?id=ED218193

Paas, F., van Gog, T., & Sweller, J. (2010). Cognitive load theory: New conceptualizations, specifications, and integrated research perspectives. *Educational Psychology Review*, 22 (2), 115–121. https://doi.org/10.1007/s10648-010-9133-8

Simon, B. (1994). Why no pedagogy in England? In B. Moon & A. S. Mayes (Eds.), *Teaching and learning in the secondary school* (pp. 16–25). Open University Press.

6 Exploring the concept of teaching transformation

> **What's our key message?**
>
> - The emergence of the Knowledge Society has necessitated a rethink of teaching and schooling to prepare students for a rapidly changing world.
> - Teaching transformation entails a shift from traditional artisan approaches to evidence-based practices, embracing new technologies and social changes.
> - The concept of "a new grammar of schooling" suggests a departure from age-related groupings and standardised instruction towards a more personalised, client-centric approach.
> - Effective teaching requires a redefinition of specialist knowledge for teachers, a focus on student outcomes, and a deeper understanding of individual student needs within the context of a Knowledge Society.

In previous chapters, we have discussed the emergence of the Knowledge Society and how it has fundamentally redefined how people work and live in the 21st century. We have provided commentary to locate the associated socio-technological changes, and we now put our finger on the need for a rethink of teaching and, in a later chapter, schooling. Our central message is that because society is changing in significant ways and because schools and teachers prepare young people for living and working in such a context, they, too, must change accordingly. Teachers cannot lose sight of the reality that young people today have different worldviews than their forebears, constituting a quite different vision for work and life. This does not mean they will not find meaning, satisfaction, and pride in their future employment. Nor that they will not need qualifications. How jobs are emerging and constituted and how people engage with them is somewhat different. Working from home, selling online, creating niche things, and working in roles such as "drone manager", "excess capacity broker", "influencer", "health and life coach", "blockchain engineer", and "ethical hacker", to name just a few, define a different world to that of even ten years ago.

DOI: 10.4324/9781003303312-8

Teachers' work contributes to who people become and their prospects; it mediates self-worth, moulds values, and orients political views. This is equally the case in public education as it is in our elite private schools. As author James Suzman (2021, p. 3) claims, our species has been shaped by a "unique convergence of purposefulness, intelligence, and industriousness that has enabled us to build societies that are so much more than the sum of their parts". The question becomes a transformation agenda: changing what of teaching and how? In this chapter, we investigate the notion of transforming teaching as a backdrop for a set of change propositions we make in the following chapters. We provide a set of key reference points that enable us to prefigure a new teacher construct and a new configuration for what is a school – what is termed a new grammar of schooling – with the aim of providing a fresh approach to the teaching agenda.

As you reflect on the agenda that the preceding chapters outlined, you realise the centrality of the role played by teachers in making transformation a reality. As the Organisation for Economic Co-operation and Development (OECD, 2018) argues, "improving the effectiveness, efficiency and equity of schooling depends, in large measure, on ensuring that competent people want to work as teachers, that their teaching is of high quality and that high-quality teaching benefits all students". The challenge for us is dealing with a legacy of issues that are the product of a system of education now well over 200 years old and a system of teaching that is captured by overcrowded curricula, contested historical and cultural positions, and a work profile that is now far too large and complex for individual classroom teachers to deal with alone. Our point is that the "teaching system", what teachers do, how they do it, and how they are prepared, needs transformation.

So, what do we mean by teaching transformation?

Prominent in the current education politics are calls for "teaching improvement". As previous chapters have revealed, there is a government narrative that decries the performance of teachers, citing declining comparative global performance metrics and, thus, the corresponding calls for improvement. "Teaching improvement" is best understood as improving what teachers currently do. While it seeks to effect improved teaching knowledge, skills, and/or behaviours that positively affect student learning outcomes, it presupposes teachers working in the same schooling context, delivering the same curriculum as they have to this point in time. As we have indicated, our world is not static.

By contrast, "teaching transformation" aims to invoke a radical rethink of teaching, what is known about teaching effectiveness, social change, and technological innovation and disruption. In addition, the explosions in understanding the brain from various fields of human endeavour, the emergence of artificial intelligence and its potential to change our world in fundamental ways, and the need to engage in more client-centric models demand new approaches to teaching that require a fit to the future. Teaching transformation moves "teacher work" into what can be called a "new grammar of schooling" and thus fits the radically different world in which people now work and live. It is built on new principles, logic, and assumptions. We explore the concept of a new grammar of schooling in Chapter 11. To understand our proposition, we pose three presuppositions that define what transformation in teaching requires and what it means in practice. First, we envision a teacher who can apply a specific body of knowledge, informed by a robust set of credible research, to teaching situations. As indicated earlier, this body of knowledge and skill defines the social status of a teacher and all of those in the profession. It sets such people apart from the amateur. This unique body of knowledge embodies what can be termed "specialist education knowledge".

Second, the knowledge base for the teacher must signify codified practice. Codification defines how teachers conduct their business and creates a framework for choosing appropriate teaching strategies and interventions. It also defines the teacher education curriculum and the assessment criteria for admittance to the profession. Having this codified knowledge thus signals readiness for work in the profession. To work outside this code would be tantamount to malpractice. We add that this codifying practice premise is not unique in the world of professional practice – for instance, medicine defines the work of doctors and engineering defines the work of engineers, but codified practice has not yet been defined for teaching. Sociologists have long called teaching a semi-profession because of the lack of a codified knowledge base that serves as a basis for professional expertise and decision-making. Codification is about defining and clarifying the practices chosen based on evidence and providing a justification for why a professional would make that choice.

Third, we distinguish between the "teacher" and the "teaching". The former refers to the qualifications of individual teachers and the requisite mix of knowledge, skills, and dispositions they bring to classroom teaching. The latter encompasses the former but necessarily refers to how teachers, students, and school organisations interact in ways that allow learning to occur. This links back to codified practice. Most reforms of the last several decades have focused on the former and much less on the latter. A first step in the transformation agenda is appreciating that the latter holds more potential in transforming teachers. Let us explain why we say this.

From artisans to evidence-based practitioners

For decades, teachers have been prepared more as artisans and craftspeople than professionals who use the science of teaching and learning informatively and execute it in consistent practice regimes. Teachers with an artisan mindset tend to be transfixed on developing and deploying creative lessons. However, these lessons often lack evidence about learning, informed instead by their predilections for children, resulting in hit-and-miss educational outcomes. They also play to "managing" cohorts and obstruct what we argue for in a later chapter: movements to "client-centric models" of schooling. The coming and going of fads and ideological bents is another characteristic of the artisan approach: if it seems like a good idea, others are using it, and it is fun, then why not embrace it? This is not the hallmark of a "professional educator". Before moving on, we raise the importance of what we mean by "professionalism" for teachers. It is of great consequence because teaching has always claimed or assumed professional status. Yet, it has not operated as a "profession" as much as it has as a trade with the euphemism of "vocation". We are persuaded that an adequate understanding of professionalism cannot be based on the attributes, characteristics, or behavioural patterns loved by education bureaucrat regulators. Those approaches represent a general indictment of the lack of professional status for teaching.

In other occupations ranked as professions, the following knowledge, skills, and values characteristics are common according to Frederic Hafferty (2023): the subordination of their interests to the interests of others; adherence to high ethical and moral standards; understanding of their social contract and response to societal needs; expressing core humanistic values such as compassion, altruism, integrity, and trustworthiness; exercising accountability for themselves and peers; demonstrating a continuing commitment to excellence; exhibiting a commitment to scholarship that advances their particular field; dealing with high levels of complexity and uncertainty; and reflecting upon their actions and decisions. Selflessness and altruism appear to be ubiquitous attitudes among experienced teachers and in attracting people to teaching. While this is hardly a negative attribute, and we acknowledge its attraction when dealing with children, our approach places a stronger emphasis on "service". The point here is that altruism and service are not sociologically equivalent concepts.

If the teaching profession is to transform as we maintain, these issues about "professionalism" are central to shifting from an immature "profession" to a fully-fledged profession. Ultimately, like medicine, it is one that will be made up of various specialisations and that will govern itself. Nevertheless, the forces of marketisation and the bureaucratic organisation of education are not about to release their control. The powers that reside in the bureaucracy of education are hardly likely to step aside and leave the field to teachers and their colleagues like ourselves. However, the vocation needs to establish professionalism as a way of organising work to deliver a better quality of education than what exists now. This is the challenge. Now, let us pause here to clarify that we are not setting out to malign our teaching workforce. It is a tough job, and teachers are dedicated people. Nevertheless, we must point out that much of what occurs as "teaching" in schools today is the product of an interplay between a prevailing long-standing culture past its use-by date and an unsuitable preparation regime. Our key point is that if we are to achieve what we believe all teachers want – every young person making the required learning gains – we must call out what we know today is not working. The teacher who counters the artisan approach uses research evidence, coupled with sets of new knowledge and skills commensurate to and exploiting a Knowledge Society era to inform practice and maximise the potential for student learning gains. These are constituent parts of what is codified practice.

However, there is a challenge because the educational research field is a somewhat disorganised body of knowledge, not to mention incomplete in many aspects, waiting patiently for someone to prepare it for teacher consumption.

Easier said than done when, as discussed in preceding chapters, one considers the contested nature of education, the scope and focus of what is researched, and the robustness of findings. Therefore, our resolution is a remaking of the education discipline and, by direct association, a new teacher construct to signal a sign-off from the past and refocus on required tasks. On a related plane, the Knowledge Society, with a proliferation of new media, artificial intelligence, and converged sets of technologies, represents yet further challenges in the teaching/schooling equation but a potent arsenal for transforming teaching and, for that matter, learning.

Let us take stock of what we have just outlined. We are saying that education as a professional study discipline is yet to find its place, having been co-opted and concocted from various other disciplines and ideological positions over recent generations. Further, an evolving set of new disruptive technology-based tools is available for teaching and learning innovation. Importantly, our view is that what is currently offered as a study in education holds little potential for codified practice or for embracing technological solutions as the knowledge base is borrowed, fluid, tacit to objectives, and captured by various ideological perspectives. Prevailing teaching "standards" – even those grounded in evidence – have evolved in a growing climate of confusion and for teachers are often difficult to implement or represent yet another "new thing" to do and consider in their busy classroom working day. In today's schools, teachers in their classrooms seem to have to know and do more, adding overload and stress to what is increasingly becoming a beleaguered workforce. Codified professional teaching knowledge, by contrast, is focused, evidence-based, has a unique language set, is practicable, and has high potential for learning outcomes. Importantly, it fosters the potential for new mindsets of commitment and pride among practitioners. This new configuration of teaching prefigures a revision to what can be understood as the scope of practice of the schoolteacher. We explore this concept in Chapter 8.

Teacher versus teaching effectiveness

Drawing on international databases, the storyline about poor and failing schools and, by direct implication, poor and failing teachers has remained static. For example, the Organisation for Economic Co-operation and Development (OECD, 2018, p. 13) report concluded that access to quality teachers and teaching continues to be "strongly related to inequities in learning outcomes between advantaged and disadvantaged students". Other researchers have found that students taught by highly effective teachers, as determined by increases in standardised test scores (using student growth percentiles and value-added measures or VAMs), were more likely to progress to higher education and earn more in their careers. As a result, the focus on the "effective" teacher continues to take on more salience, where "effective" refers to teaching – that is, instruction – what students are exposed to when in classrooms and over which schools have complete control. This points to a defined "scope of teaching practice" that can go beyond the proclivities of the individual teacher. Out-of-school factors are not ignored – they must also be addressed. However, what is signalled is a new team of "others" who work alongside teachers for the desired whole of child effects. This logic generates a rethink of what a school is and could be. Importantly for the teacher, it generates the required capacities and resources for whole student effects, allowing them to concentrate on the pedagogical elements of a refocused role in the school. The debates over what makes for an effective teacher have confounded policy and practice for too long. Let us take a quick look at how these debates have played out.

Over the decades, authors such as Gage (1963), Shulman (1986), and Berliner (2004) have laid much of the academic groundwork for current teacher research identifying behaviours and thinking that contribute to learning outcomes and how teaching expertise develops over time. Researchers have consistently identified teacher behaviours and how the use of instructional time correlates with student achievement. Other researchers have found that teacher characteristics (such as level of education and preparedness to teach) also influence student outcomes. For example, in her research review, Jennifer Rice (2003) pointed to studies that show how teacher experience, preparation programs and degrees, coursework, and certification positively impact teaching effectiveness. Other studies have shown the importance of varied qualities such as strong general intelligence and verbal ability, content knowledge, subject-specific pedagogy, understanding of learner development, and the adaptive expertise needed to determine the use of what can work given their students' needs. These lines of research have suggested that teacher qualifications strongly predict effectiveness. In a recent report, the United State's National Academy of Education argues a compelling case for more extensive pedagogical coursework in pre-service teacher education programs (Wilson, 2009).

On the other hand, other scholars have found mixed results regarding the relationships between specific teacher characteristics – for example, years of experience, type of preparation, certification status, and student achievement (Wayne & Youngs, 2003). Still other researchers have pointed out that the evidence on teacher certification is "simply too thin to have serious policy implications" (Boyd et al., 2007, p. 45). Others claim that extensive preparation is unnecessary given that teaching quality is only weakly related to readily quantifiable teacher attributes like length of training, licensure and registration status, degree, and experience levels (Goldhaber et al., 2013). No doubt education and teaching effectiveness research have gaps that must be filled. However, as Wilson (2009, p. 8) reminded us:

> The quality of teaching is not simply determined by an individual's knowledge or ability, but also by the contexts in which teachers work. Improving teacher quality thus entails policies concerning recruitment, early preparation, retention (including attention to working conditions), as well as professional development.

Too many teaching policies – from teacher preparation to professional development to compensation and career pathways – do not reflect the reality that teaching is a complex activity influenced by varied factors. We believe that no one strand of research can provide a precise roadmap for policymakers or practitioners. However, we add that research informing the field of education needs to be front and centre of such work. We do not dispute the ambiguity about the effects of individual teachers on student learning or the implications of outside factors, including school and family. Nevertheless, we believe the time is now right to redefine the effective teacher and the teaching job for the future of schooling. This definition starts with resolving what constitutes specialist knowledge for teaching and what does not. Once this resolution is achieved, preparation for teaching is refocused, creating a new teacher construct. Returning to the theme of "teaching transformation" and the future work of teachers, we cite Darling-Hammond (2022), who comments:

> Teachers need even more sophisticated abilities to teach the growing number of public-school students who have fewer educational resources at home, those who are new English language learners, and those who have distinctive learning needs or difficulties. Clearly, meeting the expectation that all students will learn to high standards will require a transformation in the ways in which our education system attracts, prepares, supports, and develops expert teachers who can teach in more powerful ways.

We contend that doing so requires a new grammar of schooling.

A new grammar of schooling

The term "a new grammar of schooling" derives from the work of Tyack and Cuban (1995), who use it to explain a movement away from age-related student groupings, the division of learning into subjects, and the standardisation of instruction that is synonymous with what young people currently experience as schooling and, correspondingly, a redefining of the role, scope, and focus of those who teach in schools. A new grammar of schooling essentially invokes a call for a change to a schooling model that meets the profile of a Knowledge Society circumstance. In a new grammar of schooling context, teachers have a deeper knowledge of their students as learners in the context of their specific learning profile. They know at an expert level what they will teach and how best to do so. Teachers have diagnostic skills to determine student learning needs and ascertain their progress – academically, socially, and emotionally – and can expertly engineer it all as positive impacts on each student's growth and development as human beings in modern society. However, not every teacher can do everything, as Basile et al. (2022, pp. xvii–xviii) state in their recent book:

> In the past, we have focused the fulcrum of change either on increasing the teacher's instructional knowledge and skill (i.e., more and more professional learning) or increasing the level of complexity of the content students must learn (critical thinking, problem-solving), and sometimes both simultaneously. Rarely do we change the role of the student or the teacher in the instructional process or the relationships between the two and others ... We need to move away from the ideology that a new program, project or activity is going to change our education systems.

At the heart of such a new system is what we call "client-centric schooling", which is a commitment to interdisciplinary teams of teachers and others who teach and work with students to achieve their individual plans for specific learning outcomes. We explore the concept of a new grammar of schooling in more detail in Chapter 8.

Towards a teaching transformation agenda?

This chapter has explored the premise of teaching transformation, describing it as a radical rethink of teaching and positioning school teaching in a new grammar of schooling that fits the radically different world in which people now work and live. Teachers are not to be blamed for the malaise of things now – just the opposite. Most school systems expect them to get racing car results but put them in an old truck to get it done. In the following chapter, we introduce a new school teaching logic and prefigure a revised role and preparation program for teachers. This novel teacher framework encapsulates the discussions thus far, indicating a departure from the educational, teaching, and schooling practices advocated in our preceding chapters, urging a symbolic sign-off on the past.

The teaching transformation agenda that is forming

- A need to remake the education discipline to better inform the preparation and the practice codes for teachers.
- A shift to evidence-based practices, incorporating knowledge from various disciplines and emerging technologies.
- The need for "a new grammar of schooling", client-centric models, and interdisciplinary collaboration for personalised learning outcomes.
- A redefinition of professionalism in teaching, emphasising adherence to high ethical standards, continuous professional development, and a focus on student growth and development in the modern world.

References

Basile, C. G., Maddin, B. W., & Audrain, R. L. (2022). *The next education workforce: How team-based staffing models can support equity and improve learning outcomes.* Rowman & Littlefield.

Berliner, D. (2004). *Expert teachers: Their characteristics, development and accomplishments.* www.researchgate.net/publication/255666969_Expert_Teachers_Their_Character istics_Development_and_Accomplishments

Boyd, D., Goldhaber, D., Lankford, H., & Wyckoff, J. (2007). The effect of certification and preparation on teacher quality. *Future Child*, 17(1), 45–68. https://doi.org/10.1353/foc.2007.0000

Darling-Hammond, L. (2022). *Possible futures: The policy changes we need to get there.* https://kappanonline.org/possible-futures-policy-changes-darling-hammond/

Gage, N. L. (1963). *Handbook of research on teaching.* Rand McNally.

Goldhaber, D., Liddle, S., & Theobald, R. (2013). The gateway to the profession: Assessing teacher preparation programs based on student achievement. *Economics of Education Review*, 34, 29–44. https://doi.org/10.1016/j.econedurev.2013.01.011

Hafferty, F. (2023). *Frederic Hafferty, PhD.* https://ches.med.ubc.ca/hafferty/

Organisation for Economic Co-operation and Development (OECD). (2018). *Effective teacher policies: Insights from PISA.* www.oecd.org/education/effective-teacher-policies-9789264301603-en.htm

Rice, J. K. (2003). *Teacher quality: Understanding the effectiveness of teacher attributes.* ERIC. https://eric.ed.gov/?id=ED480858

Shulman, L. S. (1986). Those who understand: Knowledge growth in teaching. *American Education Research Association*, 15(2), 4–14. https://doi.org/10.3102/0013189X015002004

Suzman, J. (2021). *Work: A deep history from the stone age to the age of robots.* Penguin Press.

Tyack, D., & Cuban, L. (1995). *Tinkering toward utopia: A century of public school reform.* Harvard Education Press. www.gse.harvard.edu/ideas/ed-magazine/04/03/tinkering-toward-utopia-century-public-school-reform

Wayne, A. J., & Youngs, P. (2003). Teacher characteristics and student achievement gains: A review. *Review of Educational Research*, 73(1), 89–122. https://doi.org/10.3102/00346543073001089

Wilson, S. (2009). *Teacher quality: Education policy white paper.* https://eric.ed.gov/?id=ED531145

7   A new school teaching logic

What's our key message?

- There is a need for a revolutionary shift in the role and function of schoolteachers, advocating for a new approach to teaching organisation.
- Traditional teacher preparation and roles are outdated and ineffective in addressing the challenges of modern education.
- Emphasis on a specialist approach to education, moving away from the generalist model of teaching and introducing the role of the "consultant".
- A stratified teaching workforce, including associate teachers and consultants, to better meet the diverse needs of students and optimise learning outcomes.

In this chapter, we begin a sign-off from education's past by presenting a different approach to how teaching is organised in our schools. In doing so, we create an agenda for a revolution in the role and function of what is today universally known as the "schoolteacher". The teacher makes a fundamental difference to students in classrooms. So, it is the logical place to start packaging responses to the teaching transformation agenda. Let us be upfront here. Our position is that society should no longer prepare "schoolteachers" as we understand them in our universities and colleges but replace them with a rethought teacher construct. Further, we argue that the teacher should be prepared as a "specialist in education", not a generalist with a myriad of elements unrelated to achieving learning outcomes occupying their work profile. We are not arguing that this rethought teacher construct no longer works with students directly, nor that society needs to eliminate the term "teacher". We argue that the traditional teacher construct, synonymous with teaching in our schools, has been hijacked, blinkered by tradition, distracted by all manner of industrial and ideological battles, and preoccupied with other societal issues and, therefore, has lost its way. This is a realisation for us that over past decades, fast-moving fundamental exponential changes in society have rendered the current schoolteacher construct untenable, not to mention an increasingly undesirable career choice. Think of the overcrowded curriculum, ongoing

DOI: 10.4324/9781003303312-9

negative criticism in the media, teacher role creep, increasing pressure on teachers to deal with numerous societal ills and, more recently, the emergence of new technologies like ChatGPT that enables students to "cheat" on assignments undetected. Something has got to give, and this, we argue, begins with a rethink of the "what" and "how" of teaching in our schools.

One can understand this logic when one reflects on the growth of medical doctors over time. In the early days, the doctor was the sole healthcare provider in society. They treated all patients for all things. As time passed and medical research and innovation gathered pace, a variety of paraprofessionals (speech therapists, podiatrists) and medical specialists emerged to create a healthcare system that is multi-dimensional, client focused, and specialist in nature. By contrast, the schoolteacher is primarily still positioned as all things to all students. This has to stop! This chapter is somewhat pivotal in the sequence of chapters that follow in that what is outlined herein has a knock-on effect on how our schools are organised, how teachers are prepared and, accordingly, how a significant historical and social tradition – the schooling of young people – makes a seamless and painless transition to something fundamentally different. These knock-on effects become the agenda for the chapters that follow. In effect, we begin to unpack the component pieces to illustrate the future schoolteacher. In this chapter, we front-end this exposé by identifying and explaining key contextual elements that inform such a framework.

Fundamental societal change and what it means for schoolteachers

In an era when the old cultural order of society is in flux and the labour market has restructured around knowledge industries, there is a contrast between the vision of teaching and teachers and competing opportunities – think artificial intelligence, the internet of things – that becomes starker as education systems remain locked into being organised as industrial-age bureaucracies. For example, compare "teacher" with a list of contemporary job names available online: customer advocate, influencer, career coach, internet strategist, information coordinator, personal trainer, and sustainability officer. By contrast, "schoolteacher" carries mixed cultural baggage. On balance, it is perhaps backward looking rather than future focused, without excitement about what is possible. There is little of the exhilaration, style, and movement of the creative age in teaching for most teachers. The buildings, the syllabuses, and the administrative and people management systems signal a *status quo* in the profession. The virtual absence of creative information and communication technology use pre-pandemic, frequent changes of policy direction, chronic staff shortages, the community attitudes that reinforce a vision of the past, and the seeming unresponsiveness to changing circumstances are all highlighted as symptoms of professional practice without codification.

Then there are the politics of national testing regimes and international schooling comparisons, ongoing teacher blame-gaming in the media, and societal dysfunction in classrooms, and you get a sense of how stressful teaching can be. Interestingly, teachers in Australia have a relatively high remuneration by Organisation for Economic Co-operation and Development comparisons. However, their work includes everything from bus duty to acting as a caregiver, social worker, and surrogate parent, on top of teaching the curriculum. There is simply too much going on, and the teaching role is diluted by "other things" outside their control or influence. We also contend that the current teacher education curriculum and preparation regime is unsuitable and systematically reinforces what we are attempting to reform. But more on that later. These factors contribute to a workplace under extreme duress and a profession needing a thorough rethink. Consequently, we argue for a refocusing of the professional work of the teacher away from traditional schooling-centric views, all manner of newly arrived societal obligations, and ideological evangelisms to that of a comprehensive expertise in education underpinned by knowledge and skills of the curriculum design, pedagogy, diagnostics, and evaluation tetralogy. Again, we add that we are not anti-teacher in these writings – we were once schoolteachers and school heads ourselves. Nor are we blaming them for being critical of schools and schooling when there is enough space in their day to do so. What we are saying is that we are writing this book in the hope that it can assist teachers, school leaders, teacher educators, policymakers, and stakeholders to come to terms with social change and join in the search for a more exciting and satisfying work life for our committed teachers. Not to mention dealing with the increasing rate of student underachievement in schools. As the preceding chapters have outlined, there are compelling reasons for our stance.

Top of our list is that there are few readily apparent generic attractions today in career teaching for the bright and energetic younger generations, either school leavers or middle career entrants. Such people seek professional agency and flexibility to earn a living by doing something meaningful. This meaningfulness requires focusing on applying their core skills and not having to do numerous other administrative tasks that distract from their role. In today's world, employers live or die on talent, and talented people increasingly crave fulfilling jobs that allow them to achieve meaning in their lives. Further, most employers value the growth of their talent and enact a culture of mentorship and teaming that is inherent in how work is undertaken today. It is not too fanciful to believe that the current schoolteacher role does not explicitly offer these opportunities and, in all but exceptional circumstances, schools as we know them would find it challenging to deliver on them even if it did. It is simply a circumstance of embedded myopic traditions and an over-busy workplace trumping a changed society.

These dilemmas will remain until teachers' work has a substantive and shared "futures-oriented" purpose and the teaching workplace is made more defined, innovative, creative, flexible, and appealing by better reflecting the work and organisation mores of the 21st-century Knowledge Society. A futures orientation involves the ubiquitous exploitation of all technological devices and applications for teaching and learning effects, a new set of knowledge and skills, and a corresponding mindset about how it all goes together. The next chapter explores what we mean by a futures orientation. As we said earlier, our view is that the education of teachers should be about the specialist field of education. The current teacher preparation logic is convoluted, not focused expressly on learning how to teach but distracted by a plethora of socio-political-ideological agendas, which, while perhaps valid in an aspirational society sense, are not when the goal is training people who can competently teach the curriculum so all students make the required learning gains. Note the emphasis on *all* students. Not just those who "can do" schooling. This means teachers would capitalise on an exclusive body of professional knowledge, which they would need to demonstrate personal competency for registration or certification. They would be insulated from role creep and rewarded with a strong sense of agency for their work. The teaching workplace would be organised with practices that facilitate creative problem-solving opportunities that utilise practices that rely on complex knowledge rather than opinion or ideological groupthink. There would be a requirement to operate within a codified approach to the profession, to work flexibly and in teams on innovative programs within a shared discipline environment rather than the bureaucratic conformity that has enveloped education for too long. Furthermore, they would skilfully and confidently implement programs that achieve the stated curriculum outcomes in all assigned students. This means the workplace – the school – would be client centred and thus be organised so teachers can focus specifically on teaching the curriculum. In any schooling context, there is a need for pastoral care. When we say teachers focus just on teaching the curriculum, we assume a level of pastoral care here as a vital component of the school curriculum. While the mandated syllabus in our mind will always be determined outside the school and by government agencies, the curriculum's specific interpretation and teaching to meet each student's profile will be a key operational logic in our rethought schooling construct.

Reflecting on a refocused teacher work profile means paying attention to a scope of practice applied when teaching the curriculum. On the central role played by schools in society and their place in caring for young people while parents work, one realises that the many existing schooling services provided by teachers would now not be covered. This means the modern school needs new roles, thus leading to reorganisation around multi-disciplinary teams of workers. Think of various community-based health and social work professions, technical and support staff, and various associates to teachers all working towards achieving the goals of individual learning plans. This is also about a new teacher construct.

The rise of the consultant

This type of new professional work and client engagement, outlined in Chapter 6 as "a new grammar of schooling", will require specialist coordination for specific individual student effects. Accordingly, it requires a new educational specialist we call a "consultant". We hasten to add that we argued long over what this role should be called, considering all manner of terms, such as "pedagogist", "master teacher," "learning manager", and "leading teacher", only to be challenged on terms that reflected the past. We ventured to see how medicine distinguished its experts and so settled on the term consultant, which we think invokes a set of operating logics that met our vision for such a transformational teacher role. These consultants also have a transition role in the birth of new era schooling and tea-cher education changes, which we discuss in later chapters. The role of con-sultants, which we have co-opted from the logic of how the medical profession organises its specialists in hospitals, provides complex client-centric, learning design, diagnostic and education process advice, and guidance to those "involved others" and accordingly coordinates these multi-disciplinary professionals into actioning and achieving individual learning plans. This supports the goal of scop-ing registered teacher work to just "teaching", where they work on achieving learning plan outcomes in all students. Residual schooling tasks are then redefined in the context of the "other roles" now or what we propose later should be working in schools. We hasten to add that consultants in our minds represent the career pinnacle for teachers and are achieved not through time served but higher levels of specific role-oriented formal education and the regular upgrading of their stock of complex knowledge as a matter of course, and ultimately by achieving membership of "the" pedagogical professional association. Once again, we refer-ence how medical specialists hold fellowships in specialist colleges.

There is hope for action in our vision in that schools have made significant advances in enlisting others into the schooling agenda and creating new teacher positions, such as advanced skills teachers or leaders of pedagogy, and we acknowledge this. The problem is that these initiatives have been done in a reac-tionary, add-on, and industrial way, which has only compounded the work profile of teachers as it has been done using existing competencies and an organisational and professional logic that may have fitted the 1970s but not the 2000s. Further, there has not been a narrative around who is to do what – the rescoping of teacher work – in a changed schooling context, aside from local decision-making that reacts to the latest government policy edict or seeks to engender the latest fad and encumber teachers with yet more things to do and concern themselves with.

Towards a stratified teaching workforce

With these points in mind, we propose a stratification of the school teaching workforce in our transformed schools to reflect the various interrelated teaching assignments that make up the individual students' learning plans. To this end, we envisage a scope of teaching work around associate and registered teachers, who are coached, mentored, and advised by consultants. While the premise of a tea-cher's aide is well understood in schools, the associate teacher is an advancement in this role, has the premise of a teaching intern and para-teaching professional, and can be understood more as the first rung in a stratified teaching career. Associate teachers would complete formal education, but it would be a school-based program offered in partnership with a university, and their work assignments would be commensurate to their developing teaching expertise but specifically organised to assist registered teachers with interpreting into actions learning design plans through specific teaching assignments. These assignments we envi-sage are not by way of, say, a "support into a year three class cohort context" but a fluid yet strategic arrangement of students – clients with similar individual needs – who are programmed for learning design intentions led by the consultant. Teaching assignments are tailored to directly reflect the sum of individual learning plans. Let us explore this logic in more detail.

There are two key points to make. First, we should appreciate that the school curriculum will be based on the mandated state syllabus as it is now. Nevertheless, in our minds, the school curriculum outlines what each student is to learn while at school and accordingly guides what assessment evidence is necessary, when benchmarks should be achieved and, thus, what reports are based upon to inform the next planned instruction. Curriculum planning, however, moves from homogenised age-related teaching plans and groupings to collections of individual learning plans, which, while referenced to the school curriculum for global goals, are programmed under the leadership of consultants with input from registered teachers and associated multi-disciplinary team members. This is what we term "client-centric teaching approaches".

Second, teaching work in schools consists of assignments that meet the requirements of individual learning plans and, of course, we envision there will be groupings of like plans for efficiency in many cases. However, the teacher assignment logic means students potentially being exposed to different types of teachers depending on what is to be taught and how it is to be learnt. For example, teaching assignments for associate teachers might include lesson sequences under registered teacher direction in a small group or individual student tutoring, student pastoral care, or support tasks that enable the registered teachers to focus on complex teaching assignments or associated learning plan design work.

When we mention "different types of teachers" here, we signal a sign-off from traditional classroom teachers having to teach many subjects and do many other things, as in primary schools, to arrangements where registered teachers have a focused and proven teaching competency in specific areas and are employed using differing skills for required teaching tasks. Other professionals, like associate teachers and new paraprofessionals working closely in the school, enter the scene to provide complementary services. Thus, we signal teacher education as a set of stratified qualifications and accreditations requiring teaching graduates to have a set of specialisations for study, not just in traditional subject knowledge, as in secondary schools, but specific pedagogical knowledge. We envisage teacher registration or certification being subject to a term as an associate teacher with ongoing studies in education and then demonstrating through student learning evidence that they can achieve learning outcomes in all students. Teacher registration is thus ongoing competency-based certifications, using evidence and not just time served or a judgement of others. Consultants, by contrast, would require membership of an esteemed pedagogical college after a term as "registrar" of the college, where they undergo an intensive preparation and training regime comprising formal study and in-situ coaching and mentoring by fellow consultants.

The associate teacher position is not necessarily just a phase of registration. It should be considered a career in and of itself and a key means for moving towards a more student-centric and flexible approach to schooling. We contend that registered teaching would be highly clinical and thus focused on working to ensure all make the required gains. At the same time, associates would be deployed to meet the profile of specific learning plans and accordingly take direction from registered teachers. This could include a scientist from the industry employed as an associate to teach advanced senior science, a professional netball coach for advanced sports training, or paraprofessionals who provide pastoral care or work exclusively with children with disabilities. When we mention clinical, this does not mean that teachers are aloof, robotic, uncaring functionaries devoid of warmth and rapport, quite the opposite – especially given that positive relationships are key in the teaching and learning process – but to signal a defining of specific approaches to teaching. It is a realisation that specific teaching, care, and support functions in schools are now outcomes to achieve as part of learning plans for all, with and by other professionals, and are part of the process of what it means to work according to scoped teaching work and in a stratified teaching workforce.

So, how might this all look in practice?

First, it means schools look and are organised differently. Classrooms are but one arena for teaching and learning work. Considering this new teaching workforce profile, one can imagine students having a "home teacher" to create that sense of client-centred liaison and contact, security, and organisation, which could be an associate teacher's role. Given that the school curriculum is now enacted through individual student learning plans and away from homogenous year or subject cohort allocations, the one teacher, 25 students and a closed-door classroom model now morphs into arrangements that are customised to each student's learning plan and, to this end, the consultant plays a vital advisory, coordination, and evaluation role. The environment in which teaching and learning occurs is technology rich; the use of technology is ubiquitous, mirroring how modern society exploits it for various purposes. We discuss the premise of a technology-rich teaching and learning environment and new ways of managing schools in Chapter 9. One can read its use in all the examples outlined in the following chapter.

In these types of arrangements, stratification of the teaching workforce is a key design feature, not unlike in a hospital where there are various levels of nurses, paraprofessionals, and medical practitioners. In simple terms, the technical competency of the individual team member matches the work requirement within such plans. Think of support staff undertaking routine supervision tasks, such as playground duty, first aid and set-ups, different types of "teachers" – associate teachers – working as teachers on components of agreed learning plans under the direction and guidance of a registered teacher, the teaching leaders. At the same time, consultants focus on learning diagnostics, learning designs and evaluations, and as overall coordinators. Consultants may spend time with individual students for diagnostic, review, and evaluation purposes and perhaps have a specialist teaching load, liaising with parents on critical learning plan decisions and whose advice and guidance are sought when learning plans go awry. We suggest that the registered teacher will probably remain the central, visible contact for students and parents in school life. At the same time, the consultant will be the pivot point from a rethought "system of education" perspective.

It is not hard to imagine all this when you consider how medicine started many centuries ago with just the doctor to treat all patients. Today, there is a cadre of specialists, such as neurologists, radiologists, and specific surgeons, and paraprofessionals, such as speech therapists and podiatrists, who all act in unison to treat a multitude of patient profiles. You could not imagine the doctor today being all these things, nor society expecting them to be. What a contrast to how we have positioned the classroom teacher! In most schools in developed countries, a registered teacher is employed for every 25 or so students. In our model, we envision the employment ratio of consultants, associate teachers, teachers, and the "others" now enlisted into the school to be commensurate to the sum of individual learning plans. This is important as such a model has an implicit guarantee of outcomes because the teaching workforce would be aligned to the sum of individual learning plans.

The consultant's role in conjunction with registered teachers will be to design and interpret learning plans into teaching assignments. However, the emphasis is clearly on teaching assignments and not budgets – which is the "worry" for an administrative role in the school. We discuss a rethink of school leadership in Chapters 9 and 10. This does not mean every student is taught one-on-one. However, that scope is now available to ensure everyone has the opportunity to succeed at school, as well as for strategic and corrective actions to be made promptly according to client-centric design and monitoring processes. In that light, we do not expect class sizes to extend beyond current levels. We even suggest they would lower significantly with the army of "school workers" now deployable. However, we hasten to argue that what will emerge is a system of education – a new grammar of schooling – that is driven by individual student needs. Work assignments for school staff will be allocated to the professional worker best placed to achieve specific goals. We also argue that few students will now fall through the cracks!

Let us take stock of this background before examining six concepts in the next chapter that lie at the heart of creating this new teaching construct. There are three main points we have made. First, traditional schooling and, by direct association, current teaching practices have their genesis in past social history and the various reincarnations of the state in different historical periods. Times have changed since the invention of the school in society. Second, schools and the work of teachers have become overloaded and convenient dumping grounds for dealing with societal problems, making the current teacher/schooling logic untenable and thus requiring urgent action. Third, in this historical era, there is a mismatch between teaching and learning and the patterns of work and life that now exist in the Knowledge Society of the 2000s. Moreover, knowledge about teaching and learning indicates that much is known about what works in teaching and learning but is not universally being implemented because of traditional mindsets and an out-of-date teaching and schooling organisational logic. There are parallels to teacher work in places such as TAFE colleges, universities, and training centres.

The teaching transformation agenda that is forming

- Advocacy for abandoning outdated teacher preparation methods in favour of a revolutionary shift in the role and function of schoolteachers towards a new teaching organisation model.
- Transition from homogenous school groupings to client-centric teaching approaches.
- Emphasis on the need for a stratified teaching workforce, including roles such as associate teachers to support "consultants" to cater for diverse student needs and enhance learning outcomes.
- Using the premise of the "consultant" as the goal for a rethink of the role, function, and modes of operation as well as the organisation of education work for those who work in our schools.

Part 3

Designing a new paradigm for teaching and schooling

8 New concepts for a transformation of school teaching

What's our key message?

- Key concepts for transforming teaching include emphasising a specialist field of education, codified teaching practice, workplace stratification, teachers as researchers, and teacher agency.
- Education should be a specialised domain with evidence-based teaching knowledge, moving away from the notion of teaching as art and embracing scientific approaches akin to other fields like medicine and engineering.
- Codified teaching is necessary, aiming to formalise professional procedures and techniques informed by research evidence.
- Stratification will delineate roles within the teaching profession to increase focus, expertise, and teacher agency to enhance the quality and relevance of education.

Chapter 7 focused on blueprinting a transformation of teaching work to meet the education logic we outlined and discussed in Chapters 1 to 6. The agenda for this chapter is to explore what is needed to create the teaching arrangements outlined in Chapter 7. In effect, we now unpack the inherent logic of a stratified and specialist teaching workforce to identify the concepts that give it form and function for our teaching transformation agenda. We have accordingly identified six fundamental and interrelated concepts: (i) education as a specialist field, (ii) codified teaching practice, (iii) scope of practice, (iv) workplace stratification, (v) teachers as researchers, and (vi) teacher agency. We use these concepts in a later chapter to prefigure the parts of a rethought teacher education program. We discuss each in turn:

Education as a specialist field

Our first concept in creating a new teacher construct is establishing education as a specialist field. While education is synonymous with what teachers do in schools, our message is fivefold. First, it stakes a claim on an exclusive body of knowledge

DOI: 10.4324/9781003303312-11

for teachers, and which distinguishes, by competence and through application, the professional teacher from the many others who claim to "teach". Second, it signals a clean out from current teacher education programming to create a teacher preparation curriculum that focuses exclusively on a body of specialist evidence-based professional teaching knowledge that is critical for learning success in all students. Third, and as a result of the previous, it focuses research in education faculties on the specifics of improved understandings about "applied education" and away from the side issues that have enveloped teacher education in recent years. Fourth, it lays the foundations for the process of codifying teaching practice, which we explore in the following section. Fifth and finally, is a call to action in curating the thousands of mainly small-scale and piecemeal education studies, now published, into pedagogical packages for teachers to apply and which form the foundations of codified practice – an agenda we take up in the following sections.

Let us now make a couple of arguments to locate our five points. It is common in teaching circles in schools and in teacher education faculties for school teaching work to be referred to as the art and craft of teaching. It invokes an understanding that teaching is somehow innate to the creative endeavours of the individual teacher. As such, they construct their work like an artist formulates their oeuvre. In our minds, invoking artistry like this signals that school teaching is an immature profession, creating hit-and-miss opportunities for students and their learning outcomes. An artistry logic suggests that there is no scientific body of knowledge informing it and, as such, anyone could competently undertake teaching work in our schools. This is an affront to the myriad of current teaching research evidence and the complexity of effective teaching, not to mention the profession itself. Our point is that it is time to sign off from this type of terminology, what we think is a legacy perspective on teaching, and position it rightfully alongside other noble and scientific professions, such as medicine, engineering, science, and the like. We are saying that one could not imagine doctors, nurses, or even accountants invoking artistic practices and thus freelancing outside a specific body of codified professional knowledge. Their preparation is so tight to their body of knowledge that it is only with formal preparation that the codes for practice can be understood and applied, making the pretender easily identifiable. We are not saying education should be boring. We are making the point that the instructional plans brought to bear are firmly evidence-based. To that effect, artistry is a subservient consideration, denoting preparing the required resources and creating learning environments that enable instructional plans to be fully exploited. Let us explore what this all means for those who teach.

Consider that the agenda in our schools is for all students to make the required learning gains. In that case, a focused and scientific approach to teaching, organised as codified practice, is required. Education becomes a professional domain that denotes a set of complex teaching knowledge codified – selected and organised – for professional practice. With these points in mind, education as specialist knowledge can be understood as evidence-based teaching knowledge organised through the subdomains of curriculum, pedagogy, diagnostics, and evaluation, which defines the scope of practice that we discuss later. We signal here that significant work needs to be done in curating the vast amounts of educational research in journals, books, and reports into user-friendly practice packages for teachers to use and for teacher educators to design their programs. We take up this point in Chapter 13 when discussing transition arrangements.

By invoking education as we have done, we take a decidedly overt realist position on ending the current logic of the preparation of teachers. Our new teacher construct expects that we use "graduation" as a euphemism for the successful completion of preparation for teaching, where there are multiple possibilities. Each graduate will be an expert in a quadrivial of (i) client-focused curriculum design, (ii) using learning diagnostics as the trigger point for instruction, (iii) applying the appropriate pedagogical approach, and (iv) then conducting learning and program evaluations, which are undertaken strategically to ascertain learning outcome successes. Above all, graduates will have demonstrated competence in teaching. This is the first distinction in our rethought teacher construct. The term "registered or certified teacher" is, therefore, in our minds, unequivocally focused on teaching, and they will have a proven capacity to do what they are prepared to do and are regularly evaluated on their competence with codified practices. Our consultant, as outlined in Chapter 7, is not only an extension and heightening of professional focus for teachers but also a transitionary agent in how teacher education and schools are transformed for our rethought schoolteacher logic.

There are two final dimensions to education as specialist knowledge, and these have to do with teaching content knowledge and embracing a futures orientation. Personal competence with the content taught is an essential foundation for any aspiring teaching entrant. We envision formal qualifications in applicable teaching areas as a prerequisite for entering a teacher education program. With this point in mind, we prefigure teacher education along a continuum of studies outlined in Chapters 11 and 12. The concept of a futures orientation means a personal capability to engineer an alternate teaching and learning paradigm commensurate to changes in a post-2020 socio-technological world society.

The phrase futures orientation is an aspiration for teaching graduates, signalling a new mindset of ongoing necessary social and educational vision and responsibility to embrace change. Accordingly, it signals a new set of capabilities underpinning the work of teachers. In effect, it challenges the artistry logic in teaching, replacing it with the crucial role of positively interpreting socio-technical trends and capitalising on or influencing them. This is increased teacher agency – for educational outcomes and as a learning design outcome that enables young people to transition into adulthood in a fast-changing socio-technical era. Table 8.1 illustrates the domains and associated elements for teacher work in this futures-oriented sense.

Codified teaching practice

Codified teaching practice can be understood as formalised and agreed sets of professional procedures and techniques articulated through standards that define and exemplify "accepted" professional practice. By "accepted", we mean a profession-wide agreement to move from an artistry logic to a consensus of codified

Table 8.1 The elements and domains of a futures orientation for teachers.

Futures-orientation domains (examples)	Specialist teaching knowledge base Practical, interdisciplinary, formal, applied, and contextual, including social networking capability Relevant, up-to-date, specialist in nature and "fitting"		Mindsets Individual attributes about capability and purpose	Strategic creativity Imagining, dreaming, designing, and testing with a strategic intent in mind
	Concepts	Procedures		
Futures-orientation elements	Discipline-specific knowledge Professional standards Roles and functions Teaching content Expert teaching knowledge (application of) Instruction Lifelong learning Ethics Networking and partnering Professionalism	Evidence-based practices Codified practice regime Communicating Change management Complex reasoning skills Problem-solving Planning and organising Technology application/use Strategic planning Research skills Networking and partnering	Disruptive outlooks Imagining Dreaming Agility Commitment Honesty and integrity Enthusiasm Reliability Personal presentation Commonsense Positive self-esteem Motivation Adaptability Resilience Creativity Challenging Results oriented Receptive to change/new ideas Inquiring nature Courage Intuition	**Design** Learning design process Apply professional knowledge Identify opportunity Allocate resources strategically **Diagnostics** Identify blockages and problems in systems and process Identify blockages in the process of learning: learning syndromes, learning disabilities, learning difficulties **Innovation** Creativity Problem-solving Design and test Critical thinking Calculated risk. Actively promote change

Source: Adapted from Smith, R., & Lynch, D., (2010). *Rethinking teacher education: teacher education in the knowledge age.* AACLM Press, p. 147

teaching work informed by a solid research evidence base. The intent is that in doing so, the teacher has a high chance of being successful with the diversity of clients and when to use a specific instructional device, depending on the content and the client's needs. Our point is that codified practice means specifying for teachers how different things are best taught. Further, it is an understanding that to work outside this code is malpractice, and sanctions would be applicable. Codification of teaching work accordingly informs the practice content and goals for teacher education programming and creates a framework for identifying and appraising teaching competency. Once again, this implicates the curation of educational research into user-friendly practice packages for teachers and teacher educators.

Let us pause here to locate the concept of codified practice into the fabric of teaching and schooling. In arguing for codified practice, we do not mean a return to classrooms of the 19th century, where strict rituals and levels of compliance made the learning experience frightful, not to mention counter-productive for students and the society in which they would graduate. In such approaches to schooling that were fundamentally about sorting in which a student either "made the grade" or did not, a one-size-fits-all disposition had a significant loss of human capital. The codified practice would guide teachers to strategies that create the required learning environments for all clients. Our point is that codified practice ensures we do not have hit-and-miss outcomes and that research evidence is brought to bear on practice. Accordingly, schooling moves into certainties around outcomes. We appreciate that this is a complex goal with many variables, but taking on the challenge is part of being a mature 21st-century profession. Considering codified practice, we appreciate that most education jurisdictions have developed teaching standards, and some use evidence to inform teaching from outside the profession. While we applaud the introduction of standards, we believe these standards are broadly written "practice goals" and do not define how each teaching standard should be applied. This indicates that the task of creating and implementing standards is incomplete. In other words, there is no agreed set of procedures and techniques for achieving each standard. There is silence on the teaching techniques and procedures each would require. The teaching of reading, for example, a fundamental skill that students must have to succeed at school, is universally conducted in the classroom in no discernible codified way. Each teacher essentially makes up their approach. We provide the example of the *whole-language approach* here, which has been popular in classrooms to teach reading, where the teacher's creative endeavours trump regard to a well-established learn-to-read evidence base.

This circumstance results from a dearth of pedagogical leadership, where hard decisions about codifying practice have been avoided. This leads to the decaying of teacher agency in professional and education system circles and policy arenas. However, it is also a realisation that work has not been done to curate and package the vast amounts of educational research into practice packages for teachers. Returning to our point about current teaching standards, we examine teaching standards from Australia (Australian Institute for Teaching and School Leadership, 2011). We have chosen Standard 1, "Know students and how they learn," as an example for interrogation and to make a critical point. For Australian teachers, each standard is broken down and articulated in four levels of teaching (graduate, proficient, highly accomplished, and lead), denoting what should be expected at career junctions. See Table 8.2. We will focus the point we want to make on "proficient", which is the level a graduate teacher should have achieved for full teacher registration.

Note in the proficient standard (highlighted in a black box in Table 8.2): "Use teaching strategies…". You find that because no codified practice regime informs these standards, the required teaching strategies are not detailed. Codified practice would make the teaching strategies explicit and, accordingly, the preparation regime would focus on developing the same in teachers. Instead, the artistry logic comes into play, and teachers are inclined, in effect, to make it up. Further, no codified practice regime means no guidance on the most effective teaching and no teethy framework to evaluate and improve the teacher's teaching.

Scope of practice

Scope of practice can be defined as the limit of one's knowledge, skills, and experience while also signalling what the professional is positioned to undertake and by direct association what they are not. Necessary for our discussion is that a teacher's scope of practice is situated within a code of practice and generates the need for a stratified schooling workforce. The scope of practice for our new teacher construct can be understood and, as signalled earlier, be limited to practice centred around (i) client-focused curriculum design, (ii) pedagogy and with it a focus on teaching practice, (iii) learning diagnostics to inform and ascertain the what and how of plans, and (iv) learning and program evaluation as a check on outcomes and to inform next steps. For all other schooling tasks, other roles need to be created – more on that when we explore a stratified workplace in the next section. Let us explore what scope of practice does in transforming the teacher construct in schools.

Table 8.2 An example of a typical AITSL teaching standard. Physical, social, and intellectual development and characteristics of students from the teaching standards of the Australian Institute for Teaching and School Leadership (AITSL).

Graduate	Proficient	Highly accomplished	Lead
Demonstrate knowledge and understanding of students' physical, social, and intellectual development and characteristics and how these may affect learning.	Use teaching strategies based on knowledge of students' physical, social, and intellectual development and characteristics to improve student learning.	Select from a flexible and effective repertoire of teaching strategies to suit students' physical, social, and intellectual development and characteristics.	Lead colleagues in selecting and developing teaching strategies to improve student learning using knowledge of students' physical, social, and intellectual development and characteristics.

Our earlier chapters painted a picture of overworked teachers who have suffered role creep as governments of all persuasions look to schools to solve societal problems. On any given day and as a routine of service, teachers will be involved in a myriad of tasks and activities that range from childcare to social work to event organisation and bus stop supervision. Their various roles include acting as a sports coach, parent liaison officer, dispute and problem solver, first aid officer, and welfare reporter, and too often acting as a surrogate parent. Somewhere in all this they teach, and with that, the range of what they have to teach is increasing while the time to do it diminishes with each additional problem to be solved. It is just unconscionable that this is happening in schools! This circumstance only serves to dilute the impact of highly qualified teachers and to jeopardise the life chances of young people who attend school to learn. By invoking a scope of practice, the role of the teacher is clearly defined, and the status of the teacher increases as their expertise is focused and increasingly specialist. It can be argued that the teacher becomes more engaged in this environment, and their work life and students' experiences become more attractive and positive. At the same time, those who are tasked with preparing teachers have a clear focus on what they are preparing graduates for. We assess that the current state of schooling is the product of schooling not keeping pace with a fast-changing society and teachers lacking the agency to influence policy decisions.

Workplace stratification

Stratification can be understood as the organisation and classification of a school's global set of tasks and responsibilities to a cadre of specific roles and functions and, accordingly, a rethink of responsibilities, career paths, and overall organisational work logics. As outlined in previous chapters, we envision schools being organised around a rethought teacher construct that effectively involves three levels of teachers: teaching associates, registered (or certified) teachers, and consultants. The critical point is that this stratification refreshes the current school/classroom-centric model by clarifying roles, capitalising on specialist knowledge and functions for designed effects, and creating a sense of agency for incumbents and their assigned tasks. As outlined earlier, the consultant in our education model becomes a powerful mechanism for transitioning society to this new era of schooling logic and the associated teacher preparation regime. In these arrangements, the fundamental organising principle is that each type of teacher has a specific role in achieving the outcomes of individual student learning plans and, through increased teacher agency, stewardship of schooling into the future. We add that further to such roles are a cadre of support, technical, and administrative staff who work as service providers to enable and position teachers for successful work outcomes.

Teachers as researchers

A post-2020 era society is characterised by an explosion of information and data, exponential technical innovation, including that being powered by artificial intelligence, the redefining of work and home life, and the creation of efficiencies and possibilities for solving complex problems impacting humanity. These are all products of research and innovation. The premise of the teacher as a researcher is positioning the teacher to engage with their work as an inquirer, innovator, and entrepreneur. The inquirer angle is about generating deep understandings about one's practice but also contributing to the future of education by generating and testing propositions and contributing to the education evidence base. The innovator and entrepreneur angle is a product of teacher research and an outcome of increased teacher agency in the business side of education, teaching, and schooling.

For example, the COVID-19 pandemic illustrated that web-based technologies enabled schools to move quickly and somewhat efficiently to a fully online learning environment within months under the direction of the profession. Also, the pandemic and web-based technologies essentially conspired to accelerate and consolidate the movement of university classes to online learning. These forces brought forward a generation of workers who now work predominately from home. This circumstance is a beacon for a vast array of opportunities that perhaps stand ready to offer a "value-add" to a face-to-face school day and, for the entrepreneurially minded teacher, represent the foundations for a radical rethink of schooling as a construct post 2020. The point we want to make here is that our "teacher as researcher" construct is a catalyst for change as it recognises that new knowledge is just as effective and valid when generated from those in schools and not just the academic community. Similarly, knowledge generated from the profession through solving contextual issues increases teacher agency and invokes a different but equally important contribution facilitated through partnerships between schools and universities. It can inform what it means to be schooled, how young people engage with and prosper in modern society and, from an aspirational sense, how society grows as a more favourable environment for all. Accordingly, teacher education must consider what this means for their teaching degrees.

Teacher agency

According to Priestly (2015), teacher agency concerns how teachers enact, practise, and engage with education policy. In a practical sense, teacher agency can be understood as the relative positioning and capacities, real or perceived, that teachers in both mind and body take charge of in their professional circumstances and use to influence others who impact their abilities to practise education. Teacher agency is ultimately a question about who controls the teaching profession. We argue that teachers need to be the leaders and voice in their profession and we want to enable them to be so. In the previous chapter, we commented on how role creep and government overreach have effectively stifled the teaching workforce's capacity to focus on their core curriculum and teaching business. This is a symptom of diminished teacher agency. In a rethought teacher construct, teacher agency indicates professional health and professional proprietorship. The point we seek to make here is that an increase in teacher agency is the product of a preparation and employment regime that results from a reform strategy based on engineering education as a specialist field, embracing codified practice, scoping teacher work practice to the limits and rationale of what they have been prepared for, and accordingly stratifying the workplace for efficiencies, effectiveness in better accessing expertise, and to drive professional maturity and career satisfaction.

Where to now?

This chapter has outlined the foundation concepts informing a rethought teacher construct. The chapter used references from preceding chapters to identify and explain teaching frames, concepts, and considerations that place the teacher construct at the centre of a rethought schooling arrangement. Our precise aim is to make schooling more relevant and teaching more enjoyable, effective, and significantly more rewarding for all students enrolled in our schools. Accordingly, changes are required in the "what" and "how" of teacher preparation. We trust this chapter has created an agenda for a rethink of schooling and teacher education, which is the subject of the following chapters.

The teaching transformation agenda that is forming

- A shift towards establishing education as a specialised domain, distinct from generic teaching, with a focus on evidence-based professional knowledge essential for student success.
- Formalising and agreeing upon sets of professional procedures and techniques through codified practice, informed by research evidence, to ensure successful teaching outcomes.
- Delineating the boundaries of teachers' knowledge, skills, and responsibilities within a clearly defined scope of practice, leading to a more focused and specialist approach.
- Schools organised around a stratified teaching workforce, comprising different levels of teachers with specific roles and functions, aimed at enhancing efficiency, expertise, and teacher agency.

References

Australian Institute for Teaching and School Leadership. (2011). *National professional standards for teachers*. www.aitsl.edu.au/teach/standards

Priestly, M. (2015). *Teacher agency: What is it and why does it matter?* BERA Association. www.bera.ac.uk/blog/teacher-agency-what-is-it-and-why-does-it-matter

Willingham, D., & Daniel, D. (2021). *Making education research relevant*. www.educationnext.org/making-education-research-relevant-how-researchers-can-give-teachers-more-choices/

9 Prefiguring a new grammar of schooling

What's our key message?

- New era schooling envisions schools as centres for care and wellbeing, advocating for flexible learning spaces, technological integration, and support for teachers' core teaching business.
- A transformation in education towards a client-centric model, emphasising individual learning outcomes over traditional approaches.
- A new grammar of schooling, moving away from age-related groupings and one-size-fits-all approaches.
- Redefining the role of teachers, highlighting the emergence of the specialised "consultant".

To this point in the book, we have made the case for change in education, schooling, and teaching, and accordingly identified key concepts that inform a transformation in the business of schooling and the work of teachers. In this chapter and the next, we prefigure the components of what can be understood as a new grammar of schooling. As outlined in Chapter 6, a new grammar of schooling explains movements away from age-related student groupings, the division of learning into subjects, and the "one-size-fits-all" approaches synonymous with what young people currently experience as schooling. We want to move to a client-centric model of schooling. By association, a new grammar of schooling means redefining the role, scope of practice, and focus of those who teach in schools. A new grammar of schooling essentially invokes changing the current schooling model to meet the profile of a post-2020 Knowledge Society. By positioning a new grammar of schooling as part of our teaching transformation agenda, we are, in effect, prefiguring the new work context for our transformed teacher construct.

Six key considerations constitute the new grammar of schooling we envision: (i) the school as a nursery for future citizens, (ii) engineering schools to be centres of care and wellbeing, (iii) systems to support and enable a new approach to teaching, (iv) a new model for school leadership and management, (v) the exploitation

DOI: 10.4324/9781003303312-12

of technology for teaching and learning effects, and (vi) the exploration of a new education market to stimulate innovation and disruption for futures-oriented teaching and learning impacts. To appreciate these six interrelated considerations, we have crafted five vignettes that illustrate a new logic for the new grammar of schooling we envision. These vignettes embody a client-centric schooling model organised through interrelated teaching constructs. Central to this new model is the role of the consultant. This highly specialised teacher role is at the top of a stratified teaching workforce. Also, it serves as a transition mechanism for transforming the traditional model of schooling into something more relevant to tomorrow's learners. While some vignettes may already exist in schools, we argue that a fundamental and strategic reset is needed to design schools focused on individual learning outcomes and that new teaching knowledge and skills must be learnt and honed.

Box 9.1 Vignette: Student 1

Van has been up since 5 am. He has not been able to sleep. He is too excited. It is his first day of school. Van was born with a physical disability that impacted his mobility and the manual dexterity of his hands. He has a sharp mind and has become rather adept for a six-year-old at building model aeroplanes with his occupational therapist, Trish. While attending his local school is a new experience, he is no stranger to education as he has worked with Gillian, his teacher consultant, since he was six months old and at daycare. Gillian is based at the local school and has been a critical member of his intervention team: a key person in a team of multi-disciplinary professionals. With Van about to start school, Gillian has been busy behind the scenes working with his assigned teaching team on his learning plan for his first year at school. So, Van arrives on day one at school and is met by his teacher and a host of student faces who will cross paths with him as they each encounter their learning plans. While Van might be just another face in the crowd of kids attending school, behind the scenes, he and his profile fuel an engine room of committed educational professionals ready and positioned for him to succeed.

Box 9.2 Vignette: Student 2

Across town, Vanessa, 16, having achieved sound grades while in school, now wants to follow her dreams of becoming an electrician. Her consultant has been working with Vanessa since she started in Wide Plains Secondary Network (a high school arrangement of faculties ranging from "the Arts", "Engineering and Science", "Agriculture and Horticulture" "History, Culture and Humanities" to "Robotics and Technology" and several private training providers who work under the auspices of the "partnership network" to offer specialist studies to map out her course of study). In the early days, Vanessa did not know what she wanted to do. Still, the Learning Faculty, which houses the first study program for all newcomers at Wide Plains, has been designed to focus her on learning, understanding, and positioning her talents and personal dispositions for personalised learning effects. Personal development was a favourite as it enabled her to understand and deal with mental health issues that emerged for her periodically. Her relationship with Betty, the mental health nurse, means she feels supported at school. This program also seeks to engage her in the state curriculum, which her consultant interpreted into a learning plan for Vanessa's teachers. Now Vanessa is at the stage when the option emerges for a vocational pathway, meaning a transition to the Faculty of Engineering and Science, where she will spend time studying fundamental electrical knowledge and working as an apprentice electrician with Wing Electrics. All the while, her consultant monitors progress, coordinates services, and evaluates them to ensure that Vanessa's goals are achieved. The consultant is not confined to just the school side of her plan; her consultant works with Wing Electrics, ensuring that the practical side of the learning plan is also supported.

Box 9.3 Vignette: Student 3

For Max, 12, school is both a place of learning but also a place of care. Arriving at 6 am, as both his mum and dad work long hours, he is met by Franky, the concierge at "Living Village", his suburban school. Franky is responsible for what is known as care services, and this includes things such as organising dental appointments and other health care services, as his school has been designated a government child services hub for the Living Village community; he is also responsible for Max's care, welfare, and safety while in school. He accompanies Max, who has been at the school for three years, to the breakfast room, where he meets up with his mates and readies himself for the physical activities program his consultant has recommended. Max is a keen soccer player and full of energy, and if his energy is not exhausted, he tends to get into mischief. As the clock strikes 8, it is time for indoor classes. Max has a learning profile that suggests he is an average student. A standard instruction program is deemed by his consultant to be the appropriate course of study for him at this point. However, his learning plan has identified a need for improvement in reading, so Janice, an associate teacher specialising in reading, joins him periodically for some one-on-one work. There is no stigma for one-on-one or withdrawal work, as every child at some stage finds themselves working with a variety of "associates" because education is centred on the culture of the individual and their needs. The diversity of each profile is celebrated in this school. Staying in a classroom is not a typical school day for Max. The school has been designed with various spaces depending on the subject studied. What could be described as formal learning ends towards the afternoon, when Franky arrives at the classroom door to direct Max and his fellow students to afternoon activities. After a snack break, a choice of activities is offered, ranging from swimming lessons to soccer training, or there are appointments with various services. Max's parents arrive at 5:30 pm to take him home.

Box 9.4 Vignette: Student 4

Leighton, nine years old, attends a small primary school of 50 students in a rural town four hours south of Living Village. The school comprises what can be understood as a somewhat traditional set-up with two classrooms, various withdrawal rooms, a library, an administration office, and a large sports field for outdoor activities. While outwardly the school looks like it was when Leighton's mother went there 30 years ago, what happens inside is decidedly different. Learning is orchestrated by a part-time consultant (different services are engaged based on student load), who serves a network of rural schools, supported by three school-based registered teachers and two associate teachers, who have teaching assignments based on the student learning plans. Leighton knows Miss Lee to be his "home teacher", and she is the person Leighton and his mother liaise with on teaching and learning matters and with whom he spends most of his day. He also has dealings with various teachers depending on their specialisation and the profile of his learning plan. The school is rich with technology, where specialist teachers from outside the school video conference remotely to create a blend of face-to-face and online learning events. There is no need for end-of-term parent–teacher interviews as Leighton and his mother are regularly updated on Leighton's learning plan. An online dashboard curates all daily work activities, storing information from the various platforms from lessons to show progress and providing details on teaching plans. At his school, employment positions are set within a culture of client-centred support based on the learning plans of Leighton and his fellow students.

Box 9.5 Vignette: Student 5

In a small town in central NSW, the Buglehen family, members of a religious group, homeschool their four boys. Their beliefs mean that homeschooling is the best option for the family. The Buglehens value education and want to ensure their kids benefit from a quality schooling experience. The mum, Margaret, who will be her children's primary teacher, calls on Fidel, a fee-for-service consultant, for help designing, delivering, and evaluating a learning program for her children. The education provider number that the government provides consultants funds Fidel's services and several other services, including a music teacher and access to facilities that the children's learning plans require. The provider number has transformed government funding for education, with numerous schooling options now available to families through the role of consultants. This arrangement is not unlike how governments in Australia fund general medical practitioner services. Margaret focuses on day-to-day teaching and care, while Fidel advises her, designs learning plans, and manages the logistics of services and the planning and reporting it requires.

Prefiguring a new grammar of schooling

These five vignettes are examples of a logic that underpins our call for a rethink of how schooling might be located within communities, how schooling could be organised, and how new arrangements within are brought to bear for specific student learning outcomes. If you reflect on each, ask yourself, what other profession works with clients en masse? It just does not happen because individuals present differently; a client-centric model for schooling matures the education profession beyond the generalist to specialist and acts to ensure all succeed. These five vignettes exemplify how schooling is transformed from sets of standardised homogenous age-related groupings and state-provided provisions to client-centric practice models organised through the six interrelated teaching construct concepts we revealed in Chapter 8. To recap, these are (i) education as a specialist field, (ii) codified teaching practice, (iii) scope of practice, (iv) workplace stratification, (v) teachers as researchers, and (vi) teacher agency. Recall the centrality of a new teacher construct, the consultant, in all this.

The consultant construct emerges for three main reasons. First, the role signals that highly specialised teaching knowledge is now required in our schools and, accordingly, a stratified teaching workforce is necessary. Second, in what could be called Phase 1, it operates as a transition mechanism for a system of "schooling" from one that is well over 200 years old and solidly engrained in traditional constructs and mindsets to something better able to meet the needs of the Knowledge Society. New specialist work is now required of teachers in our schools, and enabling the same in thousands of schools needs a transformation mechanism. Third, it recognises that the vast and increasing range of administrative and non-teaching related duties teachers have been required to take up is not sustainable and diminishes their capacity to apply their specialist expertise. A stratified teaching workforce means the most capable teachers with valuable specialist knowledge and skills can do what their clients need without distraction.

For the seasoned schooling operative or the informed outsider, each of the scenarios outlined in our vignettes contains arrangements that, to some degree, already exist in schools. One could say, "Hey, we are doing that already!" While we acknowledge progress, we want to react with two key points. First, schooling as we know it, with its long history and sets of ingrained traditions, acts as a powerful organisational influence on teachers, which invariably causes anything "new" to be packaged using "the old", resulting in the same outcomes but with more to do. This is the power of the status quo in education. Examples are using computers in a "pen-and-paper" environment, age-related groupings, and a six-hour day structured around bells. The consequences are an ever-increasing tail of underperforming students in age-related classrooms and calls from businesses and industry for more "job-ready" graduates. It is not a slight on hard-working teachers but a realisation that it is hard to change to something new when you have no agency; while we sense things are not as they could be, all we know (from teachers and education system leaders) is the old, normalised rituals of schooling. There is also a missing reward system that encourages such fundamental change! Here is our key message: a new grammar of schooling is a fundamental and strategic reset on the "what, when, where, why, and how" young people are to be taught the curriculum. For us, this means a design mentality focused on specific and individual learning outcome intents, taking design references from the current Knowledge Age circumstance, and correspondingly, new sets of teaching knowledge and skills must be learnt and honed by those who now teach.

Let us put all this more bluntly. Report after report call for our schools to change for the reasons Chapters 1 to 5 have outlined. Reform initiatives have come and gone. They are just not sticky enough! Many of these initiatives have been "outwaited" by cynical change-fatigued teachers, primarily because the strategy is ill-thought-out, derived from knee-jerk political actions, or represents tinkering around the edges, resulting in more complexity and ambiguity for overworked teachers. While computers adorn classrooms, technological devices and applications are not as ubiquitous as in society. In some school systems, we attempt to limit or ban new technologies. Their use adds to numerous other social change contentions not yet resolved by teachers and systems of schooling, as the old way and new way of schooling battle for primacy.

In Chapter 7, we presented an argument and a corresponding blueprint for a new school teaching construct constituted by those six concepts mentioned earlier. In effect, we sought to redefine the professional work of the teacher. Chapter 7 is pivotal in this book because the premise of the teaching improvement agenda is, in our minds, a rethink of the "school teaching construct" and the organisation of support mechanisms for such primacy to be observed and enabled. In this chapter, we prefigure what we call new era schooling pointedly as a rethought construct to support this new teacher construct. What we do not plan to do is paint a vision for a future school because a rethought school needs to fit with locational circumstances. Our vignettes are an attempt to exemplify what we now outline. If you read our outline for creating a new place of practice for a new teacher construct, you will appreciate our logic. In effect, we have identified key elements that need discussion and resolution to rethink how a new teacher construct can be enabled in our schools.

Further, one must be pragmatic in such musings because there have been massive investments in schooling infrastructure in cities, towns, and suburbs globally, not to mention the positioning of schools in the traditions, psyche, and culture of modern human life. Policymakers and alumni would not buy a call to demolish long-established community infrastructure. It is not all broken! It is essential to capitalise on what is available by focusing now on what goes on inside schools, how they should be organised for specific teaching and learning effects, and how new learning places, spaces, and circumstances should be designed for optimised student learning effects. We should not limit our thinking to the present but imagine it all into the future sustainably and seamlessly.

In penning this book, we reviewed several other practice models, such as law, dentistry, medicine, and nursing, and visited their places of work. We aimed to remove ourselves from the familiarity of schools to understand how human-centric professional practice works in other fields and see what can be borrowed or modified to rethink school operations and arrangements. We asked ourselves, what might we find here to inform our new era school? What was apparent in all the cases we examined was a clear focus on servicing clients as individuals, and we noted that each associated place of work had an equal focus on enabling the practitioners to do their specific work. There were language sets used, which we invariably could not decode and which reinforced in our mind that we were outsiders but validated our view on the role of codified practice. Designed-in features pointed to specific professional tasks being undertaken and, accordingly, who was playing what role. What was striking, though, was that multi-skilling was not a feature for the professional in these work settings. This contrasted with the school as a practice centre, in that while others are employed in a school, it was apparent that the teacher is singled out to be many things to many people. We contrasted this by observing dentists and doctors. For example, various assistants conducted preparatory tasks, enabling the practitioner to "do their professional bit". The practitioner did not proceed to wash up or assist the others in their tasks. There was a stratification of work practice and no sense of people being harried into conducting their work. In effect, professional work was left to a code of practice where professional and support functions operated accordingly. Those supporting were also trained, and one could see that rituals and routines were complementary to an obvious code of practice.

The other striking feature is that clear professional parameters were at play in these practice situations. For example, we observed a child who categorically refused to sit in the dentist's chair. It was not a matter of fear but a stubborn refusal to stop playing a game on his mobile. No manner of cajoling or bribing could convince the child about the benefits of good oral health. The dentist did not enact a sanction for such behaviour and nor did he remove himself to an office to begin plans for a behaviour management strategy. He said, "Take your child home, and when he is ready, make another appointment". His scope of practice did not extend to errant behaviour. His practice was dentistry and nothing else. We are not saying this should be the attitude of schools – quite the opposite – we are saying here that what makes schools unique and valuable in society is that they have a charter to deal with the whole child. Our point is that dealing with the whole child does not mean it is exclusively dealt with by one teacher.

With these points in mind, we now explore the six grammar of schooling considerations we introduced in the opening section of this chapter. We will further expand on these in the following chapter. While we discuss each in turn, commencing with the concept of schools as a nursery for future society, we must add that each has a certain interplay with the others. Accordingly, they should be read with the others for insight into the overall look and feel of new era schooling. Further, as you read the design features of each one, you need to superimpose the new professional logic Chapters 7 and 8 outlined, where teaching work now comprises a stratified multi-dimensional teaching staff. Accordingly, you will begin to appreciate the premise of this book's teaching transformation agenda.

A nursery for future citizens

Let us be upfront here: our new grammar of schooling logic is principally a place of learning. Its key charter is to teach the state curriculum and prepare young people for a future society. One needs to appreciate that for modern society to work, schools have care functions and many moving parts. Our point has been that teachers teach, and there needs to be others who do the "other things", not about teaching. The term "nursery for future citizens" is thus apt. Still, as our following commentary outlines, there is a certain sophistication in schooling structures that profoundly impacts the product of schools and invariably influences what teachers do and how they choose to do it. The point here is that being aware of them is the first step, while the second is deciding what should be constituted for the required effects.

Despite their long history and easily recognised traditions, we argue that schools will exist long past today because they are invariably the last visible and viable "community centre" in modern society and, importantly, act as a nursery for future citizens. What we are saying here is that while there will be opportunities for alternatives to classroom learning through technological innovations and disruption, the reality is that schools as physically located places for young people in a community will continue because they provide levels of care while both parents work and because a mechanism is still needed for preparing and inducting our young people into society. Our message is that schooling plays a vital role in shaping the cultural fabric of society, contributing to the creation of a shared cultural identity and developing essential knowledge and skills in young people. It is now time to revisit it, not for revision's sake, but in the realisation that young people are growing up and participating in a different world, characterised by many new opportunities and ways of doing things, but also in a context of contested positions which require resolution. Let us explore this now in more detail.

In Chapter 5, we discussed what it means to be educated. We painted a picture of exponential technological innovation and change, creating new circumstances in society that now require resolution. We theorised the points of resolution around the need to answer the question: "What does it mean to be educated today?" We provided a series of key considerations and sought a discussion frame for society and the teaching profession to jointly resolve this question and interpret and locate the teaching of the state curriculum. Answering such a question is also a strategy for the preliminary design work needed for new era school development. It is about buy-in as well as being fit for purpose.

While the school's formal curriculum outlines key knowledge and skills to be learnt and honed for later life, schools also enact what can be called the "hidden curriculum" – a set of designed-in arrangements and ways of doing things that transmit cultural values, beliefs, and norms from one generation to the next. This plays an essential role in shaping the cultural identity of young people and influencing their perceptions of the world around them. Schools mould and induct young people into society. This "induction" is achieved by creating a shared sense of history and cultural heritage among members of a society and by providing opportunities for students to interact with individuals from diverse cultural backgrounds, fostering an understanding and appreciation of cultural diversity. Schools help break down cultural barriers and promote a more inclusive and pluralistic society by promoting intercultural communication and understanding. Furthermore, schools perpetuate cultural traditions through curricula and extra-curricular activities, such as religious events, music, sports, and arts programs. These programs expose students to their community's cultural heritage, helping preserve and promote traditional cultural practices and values. They also enact rituals, such as parades, salutations, uniforms, and observances, which further reinforce the socialising agenda of the school. The question is, is it all still relevant or necessary?

Failing to incorporate cultural and socio-cultural perspectives into the conceptualisation and design of modern education, solely focusing on academic pursuits, neglects the vital role schools play in society and overlooks the comprehensive objectives and responsibilities they should fulfil. While we have spoken of a long tail of underachievement in academic areas, this tail also refers to the lost opportunities for many young people who drop out of our schools and dwell on society's fringes. The challenge lies in establishing and mobilising a consensus on the definition of education in the post-2020 era and implementing agreed-upon principles to accomplish these objectives. As we have said, we hope the concepts highlighted in this book guide where to start and what to consider. This rethink is captured through the goal of client-centred learning provisions, new and aligned professional practice regimes, and society-wide resolutions on what it means to be educated in a post-2020 world.

The model for teaching and schooling outlined in this book is best understood as matching service provisions optimally to individual needs. While invoking the "individual" in this context is a deliberate teaching design logic, we are careful to point out that schooling cannot be all about the individual. Being a member of society means learning how to be an individual in a group of other individuals. So, any future schooling construct cannot avoid invoking the hidden curriculum. The hidden curriculum needs to be a product of answering what it means to be educated today for tomorrow.

Centres for care and wellbeing

In early times, children in the West attended a school sponsored by the local community and arrived home to mothers acting as homemakers. Only fathers worked, and the premise of care and wellbeing fell to religious adherence, doting parents, and extended family members. Schools of the times were expressly places of learning and focused routinely on the basics and instilling, at least in the West, virtues spelt out in the bible. *Loco parentis* was understood as a sense of entrustment in the absence of parents, but when things went awry, Mum and Dad were local and quick to respond. Fast forward 50 years to 2024, and the notion of family life and community has come to mean very different things. Invariably, both parents work, so care requirements for young people extend beyond school hours to times before and after and expand beyond "keeping them safe" to facilitate their wellbeing. Community is understood more in terms of engaging in an online platform or attending staged events, often outside where one lives. What may not have changed much is what happens in and around the school, especially in rural and remote locations, making it very often the local community centre. In more recent times, mental health has come into sharp focus as a once-hidden struggle for many young people in society. As an example of a wellbeing strategy, schools, with their community-centric logic, now represent opportunities for helping and enabling young people to travel into adulthood. This change signals the premise of schools as "one-stop-shops" for community service provisions, reinforcing the need for schools to be designed as having face-to-face components and centres for para-professionals to work in unison with teachers for individual student health and well-being effects. This is often described as a school offering "wrap-around" services or a "service hub".

The school day needs to be rethought, and the buildings resourced as potentially 24/7 establishments, where dimensions of care range from "childminding" to education to health and wellbeing, not as a disconnected service provision but as multi-dimensional community-based service provisions that parents and care-givers can opt in or out of. The services accessed would depend on the learning plans enacted by their child's consultant and the teams engaged. These indications underscore schools' evolving role in caring for young individuals. Consequently, schools must carefully consider the "what" and "how" of our educational approach.

In all the arrangements outlined here, decisions on the overall wellbeing, growth, and development of young people remain in the parent domain. There is no suggestion that the state now overreaches into the family to take charge or that kids spend most of their time in schools. We are saying here that society has changed, and with it, new circumstances have emerged that need to be designed and considered. New era schooling is thus about and is built on a partnership with parents, where the latter seeks advice and service provision from the former as a component of how people parent their children today. Responding to parental requests is the school's domain, and the coordination and provision of services are now under the direction of a new construct in a multi-dimensional team. One can easily conceive accountability for educational outcomes moving from a "hands-off" remote bureaucracy to a "hands-on" local professional educator with client-centric accountabilities. We call this innovation the consultant.

Supporting and enabling teaching

The concept of new era schooling is built on a simple logic that emphasises the importance of teachers in the student's learning process. In traditional schools, teachers play a fundamental role in the education of students, and this remains true in our view on new era schooling. However, in new era schooling, teachers are freed from time-consuming, secondary to teaching tasks and provided with more specialised client-centred teaching assignments. This requires making it essential to provide teachers with new levels of strategic support and enablement. First, supporting and enabling teachers in new era schooling means that the school environment will differ regarding where, when, and how teaching and learning occur. While classrooms will still exist, they will be designed as new spaces and places with new times for teaching and learning. This will all be engineered to suit the needs and profiles of client students – meaning that new era schools will provide a more flexible and personalised learning experience for students, allowing them to learn in a manner that best suits their needs. Second, the head or principal of the school will need to concern themselves chiefly with advocating for and marshalling resources and arrangements that enable and support the teaching work logic. The head will be responsible for ensuring that all the working parts of the school do so harmoniously together and project a sense of purpose and relevance. This includes providing teachers with the necessary resources, such as materials, equipment, and technology, to support their teaching work and ensure they meet their students' needs. Third, heads of new era schools will relinquish their pedagogical leadership role to the school's consultants. Consultants are positioned to practise as lead specialists in an "education" process organised through client-centred learning designs, assessments, and evaluations. This approach means that administrative tasks trigger the need for "deputy heads" or "managers" who work to enable teachers to focus on their core business, freeing them from distractions or future role creep. Finally, supporting and enabling teaching in new era schools signals a harnessing of technology for teaching and learning effects. New era schools should view technological devices and innovations, including artificial intelligence, as opportunities. Teaching and learning logics such as blended learning provide insight into how new era schooling might support the business of teaching and, accordingly, how it exists in society. Using technology to enhance teaching and learning, new era schools can provide students with a more efficient, effective, and personalised learning experience. These dimensions are summarised in Table 9.1.

New era schooling is built on a simple yet powerful logic that moves mass education approaches to client-centric models, emphasising the importance of teacher agency in the student's learning process. It rethinks schooling of old around a clear focus on teachers applying specific education knowledge for individual student learning outcome effects. However, it also presupposes a new way of organising teacher work beyond the classroom teacher having to be all things to all students. By supporting and enabling teachers, providing flexible learning spaces, and using technology to enhance teaching and learning, new era schools

Table 9.1 Dimensions of the new era of schooling.

Dimension	Explanation
Importance of Teachers	Teachers are the most important factor in student success, so a new era schooling construct should be built on specialised teaching assignments that are resourced, supported, and enabled.
New Learning Spaces	While traditional classrooms will still exist, new era schooling should involve new spaces, places, and times for teaching and learning tailored to the needs of different locations, teachers, and students.
Role of Head/ Principal	The head/principal's role should shift to advocating for and marshalling resources that support teaching work logic. They should ensure that all working parts operate harmoniously and with purpose. Pedagogical leadership would be delegated to a cadre of consultants with expert knowledge and skills and specialising in client-centred learning designs, assessments, and evaluations.
Administrative Tasks	Administrative tasks should be delegated away from teachers so they can focus exclusively on their core teaching business.
Harnessing Technology	Technology and innovations like apps and artificial intelligence should be viewed as opportunities and harnessed to support teaching and learning, including blended learning approaches.

can provide students with a more personalised and effective learning experience. While some will argue that our schools are already doing this, we retort that the orchestration of pedagogical frames and workplace stratifications this book has designed into our new grammar of schooling are absent in such claims. Alternatively, more globally, we support Hannon and Peterson (2017, p. 11), who argue, "There is no clear narrative or unifying ambition for public education today that both connects with the realities that people are experiencing and which faces up to what can confidently be said to be our horizon". As we move into an increasingly complex and competitive world, providing a high-quality education to students cannot be overemphasised. New era schooling provides a framework for achieving this goal. Chapter 10 outlines the new grammar of schooling considerations by dealing with (i) technology-rich environments, (ii) a new model for school leadership and management, and (iv) the education market.

The teaching transformation agenda that is forming

- A new grammar of schooling is a fundamental and strategic reset on the "what, when, where, why, and how" young people are to be taught the curriculum.
- It needs to be a place where young people are positioned and supported – educated – to be future citizens and not inhabitants of a world now long past.
- Care and wellbeing are now fundamental considerations in a new world characterised by ongoing and fundamental exponential social change.

- A new grammar of schooling requires a new set of teaching support enabling features providing teachers with necessary resources, administrative support, and technology integration to enhance teaching effectiveness and focus on core teaching responsibilities.

Reference

Hannon, V., & Peterson, A. (2017). *Thrive: Schools reinvented for the real challenge we face.* Innovation Unit Press.

10 An expanded focus for schools

> **What's our key message?**
>
> - Technology-rich environments are crucial in modern schooling, offering opportunities for varied learning paths, adaptive instruction, and immersive experiences through e-learning, collaborative tools, assessment methods, and educational software.
> - New school leadership and management models emphasise a client-centric approach, restructuring roles and decision-making processes to support individualised student learning needs and empower teachers as professional practitioners.
> - Educational transformation requires strategic visioning by system leaders, advocating for policies that integrate technology, enhance teacher training, and foster research-informed practices, alongside investment in infrastructure and professional development.
> - The evolving education market embraces technological integration, personalisation, global accessibility, lifelong learning, diverse learning environments, and entrepreneurial approaches, offering both challenges and opportunities for reshaping education delivery and experience.

In this chapter, we continue our exploration of "a new grammar of schooling". While Chapter 9 dealt with what can be described as new support and enabling considerations, this chapter focuses on a set of systems that give body to the operations of the new grammar of schooling: (i) technology-rich environments, (ii) a new model for school leadership and management, (iii) new education systems thinking, and (iv) the education market.

Technology-rich environments

A technology-rich learning environment refers to an educational setting, both the physical and virtual arenas where technology is integrated meaningfully and purposefully to support the work of teachers and enhance teaching and student

DOI: 10.4324/9781003303312-13

learning. The premise of a technology-rich environment contrasts with traditional schools where pen-and-paper teaching and learning regimes still predominate. A technology-rich learning environment aims to create a dynamic and engaging educational experience that leverages technology to support teachers' and students' learning in new and innovative ways. When thinking about how ubiquitous technology is in society and the various devices, software platforms, and applications available, one can imagine the new era schooling as exploiting technology in the following ways:

- E-learning: Online course materials, educational videos, and virtual field trips are examples of how technology is used for e-learning.
- Collaborative tools: For example, Google Classroom, Blackboard, and Edmodo foster interactions between students and teachers. Stack, monday. com, and other platforms change the way teachers collaborate, manage workflows, and centralise information and data sharing.
- Assessment and evaluation: Technology-based assessments measure student understanding and provide instant feedback to students and teachers, including providing diagnostic learning information.
- Educational software and applications: Kahoot, Quizlet, and Socrative provide interactive and engaging ways for students to learn.
- Data tracking and analysis: Data dashboards and analytics software allow teachers to track student progress over time, understand the impact of teaching, and adjust their methods accordingly.
- Adaptive learning: Technology-based adaptive learning systems can personalise instruction and offer customised learning paths to meet the needs of individual students.
- Virtual reality, augmented reality, and simulation provide students with powerful, immersive learning experiences.

While calls for the use of technology in classrooms are nothing new, and the ways of using technology are used to varying degrees in classrooms today, the point we make here is twofold. First, technology offers a myriad of potential opportunities to deliver the curriculum by allowing teachers to vary the path, pace, and place of learning and enhance their potential to deal with students as individuals. Second, leveraging technology bridges the gap between the traditional schooling experience and the contemporary world, reflecting the pervasive presence of technology and its advantages in home and work environments. It also acknowledges that the modern Knowledge Society inherently relies on technology, thus shaping future society. In addition, it implicates the technological skills underpinning teacher work and the "what" they need to be prepared for the new era school.

On a parallel plane, technology repositions teachers regarding research, development, and innovation. Teachers can no longer be positioned just as consumers or technology users; they must be positioned differently and thus trained to be contributors by acting as researchers and education field contributors and, therefore, navigators for where technology can and should take the profession into the future. A still further realisation is that teachers must take their optimised place in society, and new era schooling must come to mean enabling and supporting them.

New school leadership and management models

A theme has begun to emerge as we position the teacher as a critical player in a multi-dimensional teaching workforce within a new grammar of schooling. This theme is a movement towards client-centric approaches and enhancing teacher agency in the decision-making process as the central organising feature. This is a fundamental shift from age-related classroom groupings and mindsets that create considerations where teachers are obliged to consider themselves as "all things to all students" and the school's administration as a centre of maintaining conformity. The complexity of modern life, the expansiveness of curriculum, and constantly changing socio-political schooling landscapes make standardised and solo teaching assignments nearly impossible, not to mention inefficient. We have thus invoked the medical model where multi-disciplinary teams can access specialist expertise, in conjunction with stratification of roles, generating new teaching capacities and a flipping of education planning from curriculum-centric plans for cohorts to individual student plans referenced to curriculum requirements.

This new client-centric approach causes the school's leadership and management functions to become more enablers and supporters of teaching work. While one could argue that current school leadership and management arrangements have this as a goal, the reality is that schooling as a mass activity needs different organising principles. In the existing model, we seek conformity, consistency, and commonalities to ensure a sense of organisational structure and control, in contrast to new arrangements that will build on localised customisations and decision-making for each student. School leadership and management in client-centric arrangements are best understood as a professional practice leadership and management model. A stratified workforce operating within a multi-disciplinary team requires decision-making processes within the context of and in direct reference to individual clients rather than the overall school. The leadership system is sustained within the stratification of professional expertise, while the management of associated systems becomes positioned to support decisions made. This is a fundamental movement from principals and executives as the decision makers to the practitioners enacting a professional practice model. There is a parallel here with how the medical profession is organised, with the leadership focused on supporting client-centric decisions. In our school model, the primacy of teacher agency in teaching work is confirmed.

New systems in education

The teaching transformation agenda envisages an ambitious overhaul of the education system, requiring new strategic insights and a nuanced understanding of how to create the conditions for teachers to maximise student outcomes from system leaders. This section focuses on system leadership's pivotal role, which involves re-envisioning schooling and practically implementing transformative changes. At first glance, adopting a "greenfield site approach" – starting afresh – might seem more straightforward and practical. However, considering the enormous scale at which entire education agencies must implement such changes, this approach might be impossible. As Ivan Illich (1971), famous for authoring *Deschooling Society*, proposed, if you want to change a complex system with deeply embedded ways, you will not do it from revolution or reformation – you need to tell a compelling alternative story – a new narrative.

At the heart of this educational transformation lies strategic visioning. System leaders must devise their understanding of the future of learning and articulate a clear and compelling purpose for schooling that resonates with the messages highlighted in this book. This vision for transforming the teaching agenda should articulate a comprehensive overhaul of teaching practices and curriculum design, the integration of cutting-edge technology, and a fundamental restructuring of teacher education. System leaders must articulate this vision and inspire commitment from the educational sector and the wider populace. Such a vision must bridge the gap between current educational realities and the future's demands, rallying all stakeholders around a shared objective of transformative change.

However, a vision without action is merely a dream. Therefore, system leadership must actively turn this vision into tangible initiatives through policy innovation, advocacy, and enabling increased professional agency. Such innovation recognises old models of change that relied too much on top-down direction actioned through accountability and cohesion. The mindset that engineering changes from above through the drive for effectiveness and efficiencies should be left to the industrial age. To facilitate meaningful change, leaders should collaborate closely with a broad spectrum of stakeholders – including educators, policymakers, industry experts, and community representatives – to develop more sophisticated approaches and frameworks that actively support, rather than control, those that ultimately drive the transformative journey. Revising existing policies and practices to get teachers and school leaders to work harder will not be effective. True transformation requires advocating for policies that align with, actively guide, and accelerate the adoption of the new teaching models presented in this book. This involves a nuanced understanding of the unique challenges and opportunities presented by contemporary educational landscapes. System leaders should advocate for policies that enable the seamless integration of technology in education, recognising its pivotal role in modernising teaching and learning environments. This approach should also include creating new structures in teacher education, ensuring that future educators are equipped with the skills, knowledge, and mindset necessary for success in this rapidly evolving domain.

Following the policy environment, a crucial aspect of educational transformation is the focus on professional development and capacity building. System leaders must advocate for and reconceptualise teacher training programs, aligning them with the new teaching constructs in this book. The current roles and designations in schooling do not adequately align with the transformation agenda. Instead, a more specialised and codified approach is necessary, particularly in this era of personalised learning. While there is a differentiated focus on teaching methods from the early years to secondary school graduation, this approach demands a significant enhancement of skills in "diagnosing" student learning needs at their stage of development. Moreover, specialised teaching strategies tailored to specific academic disciplines are essential. This specialisation goes beyond traditional subject knowledge, encompassing innovative pedagogical strategies that cater to diverse learner needs.

Additionally, a strong emphasis must be placed on research-informed practices. The new teams of teachers outlined in this book should be equipped to apply the latest educational research in their classrooms and critically evaluate and contribute to this body of knowledge. This dual role as practitioners and researchers empowers teachers to continuously evolve and adapt their teaching strategies, ensuring they remain relevant and effective in a rapidly changing educational landscape. The cornerstone of the "new teacher" role in the transformed educational landscape is a strong emphasis on data utilisation. Informed decision-making, grounded in robust data and research, is crucial for the success of the teaching transformation agenda. System leaders hold a crucial position and should prioritise using advanced assessment tools, extending beyond standardised tests, and gauging the efficacy of novel teaching approaches and educational reforms. This data should then be used to refine and improve educational strategies continuously.

A specialised data ecosystem should be developed for education to mirror the medical profession's use of test results in diagnosis and treatment. Such an ecosystem would provide consultants and their teachers with comprehensive insights, allowing them to clearly articulate and plan the next steps in a student's learning journey. This approach extends beyond academic achievement; it encompasses various aspects of student development, including emotional wellbeing, social skills, creative aptitudes, and other critical competencies. Furthermore, this data-driven approach should not be static; it must evolve to keep pace with the changing educational landscape. System leaders should ensure that these data ecosystems can incorporate new metrics as our understanding of effective teaching and learning deepens.

In their redefined roles, teachers must be adept at interpreting this data, discerning underlying patterns and translating these insights into actionable strategies tailored to each student's unique needs and learning path. Professional development programs should thus include training in data literacy, ensuring educators can harness data's power effectively. Since the data and its analysis are vehicles for student learning decision-making, teachers must deeply understand qualitative and quantitative data analysis. This expertise allows them to interpret test scores, assignment results, and other student feedback forms effectively. They must be able to identify trends and anomalies within this data, which can provide critical insights into a student's learning process, strengths, and areas for improvement. With this knowledge, teachers can make informed decisions about instructional strategies, curriculum adjustments, and personalised interventions. The ability to act upon data with precision and insight is essential for fostering this new learning environment that adapts to and meets the needs of each student.

To fully grasp the breadth and depth of what is required, transformative education demands not just visionary ideas but a concomitant investment in appropriate resources and infrastructure. System leaders are pivotal in ensuring schools are comprehensively equipped for this new educational paradigm. This requirement extends beyond standard school necessities; it encompasses a wide array of essential components, including but not limited to skilled personnel adept in modern teaching methodologies, state-of-the-art technology tailored for educational purposes, and dynamic digital platforms that support innovative learning and teaching strategies. Infrastructure investment represents more than a financial commitment; it is a foundational pillar for creating interactive, adaptable, and responsive learning environments. These environments are crucial for supporting the innovative teaching and learning strategies at the heart of educational transformation. Such an investment involves outfitting classrooms and teachers with advanced technological tools and resources. Infrastructure investment should create physical and virtual spaces encouraging collaboration, critical thinking, and creativity. This means reimagining classroom layouts to promote group work and discussion, equipping spaces with tools for creative expression, and designing areas that support hands-on, experiential learning. In this context, system leaders must also prioritise and invest in the professional development of educators, ensuring they are comfortable using these technologies and skilled in leveraging them to enhance student learning outcomes.

A new education market

The term "new education market" refers to the evolving landscape of educational services and products in response to technological changes, society, and economic demands. The scope of any new education market, especially the compulsory schooling sector, will be primarily determined by prevailing government policies and the degree to which government funding to schools is liberated for entrepreneurial effects. Aside from that, a new education market can be appreciated as a dynamic and rapidly evolving sector, reflecting broader shifts in technology, society, and the economy, and chiefly as a response to gaps between socio-technical change and workplace and homelife consistencies and learning needs. Several key features characterise this market. Table 10.1 provides an insight into potential new market outcomes.

Creating and contributing professionally to a new education market represents a promise to reshape how education is delivered and experienced by people in the coming decades. It also creates a set of motivating circumstances that encourage innovation and disruptive teaching and learning work. While new education markets have the potential to change education systems like what we have outlined as a new grammar of schooling, it is both a challenge and an opportunity for those who currently work in schools. This is because a new education market, beyond the controls of current government funding, presents a new set of operating requirements that mandates new expertise and mindsets for success. There needs to be a break away from the environment of increasing accountability and

Table 10.1 New education markets.

Technological Integration	Digital technologies, such as e-learning platforms, software applications, and online resources, play a central role. This includes using artificial intelligence, virtual and augmented reality, and adaptive learning systems.
Personalisation and Customisation	There is an increased focus on meeting individual learning needs. This means offering personalised learning paths, adaptive learning experiences, and customised content that caters to different learner profiles.
Global Accessibility	Education is increasingly accessible across geographical boundaries, thanks to online learning platforms and digital content. This globalisation of education allows for cross-cultural learning experiences and international collaboration.
Lifelong Learning	The new market caters to traditional Kindergarten to 12, higher education, adult learning, and professional and personal development. Lifelong learning is emphasised to keep skills relevant in a rapidly changing employment market.
Diverse Learning Environments	Beyond the traditional classroom, learning environments now include online courses, hybrid models (combining online and in-person learning), and experiential learning opportunities such as internships, inquiry, and project-based learning.
Entrepreneurial and Innovative Approaches	There is a trend towards entrepreneurial models in education, with startups and new businesses offering innovative educational products and services.

competition for scarce resources. It requires adaptation to embrace new technologies and teaching methods, invest in digital infrastructure, and rethink traditional educational models. Importantly, it also offers the potential for more personalised, effective, and inclusive education.

The teaching transformation agenda that is forming

- The teaching transformation agenda aims for a comprehensive overhaul of the education system, including the integration of cutting-edge technology, restructuring of teacher education, and adoption of client-centric approaches.
- System leaders play a pivotal role in articulating a clear vision for transformative change and turning it into tangible initiatives through policy innovation, advocacy, and increased professional agency.
- Educational transformation emphasises research-informed practices, data utilisation, and investment in infrastructure and professional development to support innovative teaching and learning strategies.
- The emergence of a new education market reflects shifts in technology, society, and the economy, offering opportunities for personalised learning, global accessibility, diverse learning environments, and entrepreneurial approaches to reshape education delivery and experience.

Reference

Illich, I. (1971). *Deschooling society.* Marion Boyars Publishers. https://monoskop.org/images/1/17/Illich_Ivan_Deschooling_Society.pdf

11 Preparing a new teacher construct for a new grammar of schooling

> **What's our key message?**
>
> - A transformative agenda for teacher education programs to adapt to the changing landscape of schooling in the post-2020 era requires a rethink of teacher education.
> - Current models of teacher education reinforce a replication of traditional approaches to teaching and schooling. There is a need for a client-centric approach, evidence-based practices, and a focus on bridging the gap between theory and practice.
> - Transforming teacher education starts by creating reference points which point to a transformative teacher education program experience. This means a new set of guiding principles and program organisers come into play, from which teacher education is designed.
> - Collaborative partnerships between universities and schools will create a more effective and attuned teaching system.

The time has come in our book to outline our thinking on preparing a new teaching construct. Early on, we clarified that our goal in writing this book was to seed a transformation of teaching in our schools. In summary, chapters to this point have examined an interconnected set of fundamental societal changes that have redefined what it means to work and live in the post-2020 era. Our discussions have focused on the role played by schools as a system for preparing young people for such a circumstance and, accordingly, a set of propositions for how the concept of schooling should be refocused and reorganised has been outlined. Central to these propositions is a new role and focus for those teaching in schools. Our discussions through the book show the centrality of the teacher – what they do and how they do it – and their positioning within a rethought schooling system. In effect, we have signed off from the teacher organisational and operational logic of the past. We have set an agenda for new teacher types and their positioning within a multi-disciplinary team operating in a new grammar of schooling. This can be best understood as

DOI: 10.4324/9781003303312-14

futures-oriented, evidence-based, client-centric approaches to education in our schools. We have compiled these key findings from previous chapters into Table 11.1. This table focuses on transformative teacher education program aspirations. The pivot point for achieving our teaching transformation goal is rethinking teacher education, and we now take up this challenge.

Key teacher education program elements

In our view, in reference to Table 11.1, teacher education programming should be framed around seven key elements. First is teacher work in the context of a stratified teaching workforce and a defined scope of practice for each interrelated teaching role. These two components are the foundation of what teaching work is and what it is not and, by direct association, how schools and teacher work are organised for required teaching and learning impacts. The content informing such "new" work is based on a renewed education knowledge base derived from what we conceptualised in Chapter 8 by defining education as a specialist field. This body of specialist education knowledge will have a credible pedigree of research evidence and practical protocols that create a high degree of certainty about its effectiveness in achieving desired learning outcomes in learners, no matter their circumstances. Student teachers will then learn this specialist knowledge in a rethought theory/practice arrangement and present it through the lens of codified teaching. Codified practice is a model for how specialist education knowledge is practised, and it works to illustrate how teaching is undertaken and, thus, how learning outcomes are achieved. It also differentiates the expert teacher from the amateur in practice circumstances. More specifically, it is formalised and agreed-upon sets of professional procedures and techniques articulated through standards that define and exemplify "accepted" professional practice. We follow Noel Pearson (2006) and John Hattie (2016) from Australia in proposing that instruction is the key factor in determining teacher quality and codified practice, moving the profession from artistry mindsets to evidence-based practice regimes and more certainty for learning outcomes to be achieved in all students.

These teacher education elements create a foundation for higher states of teacher agency in educational decision-making and contribute to a rethink of how schooling is conceptualised, organised, managed, and led. A final element is future-proofing the teacher role by instilling an innovation and disruption teaching mindset as part and parcel of the work of teachers, given that the world in which we live is in a constant state of change. Teacher work needs to harness the potential of location and entrepreneurialism by positioning teachers as researchers. Having made these preliminary comments about our seven teacher education programming elements, we now expand on their collective premise by locating them within a context of current and future teacher education programming.

Table 11.1 Teacher education program goals (based on works by David Lynch).

Program design goals	Teacher education program focus	The basis of our organising idea
1. Stratification of the Teaching Workforce	The *type* of preparation programs required.	·A redefining of teacher and teacher-related work assignments in the school, which represents a rethink of "who does what" in the school defined as responsibilities, career paths, and the overall logic of organisational assignments.
2. A Scope of Practice	What the teacher must be able to do once employed.	·A defining of what is teacher work and what is not and who else (e.g. paraprofessionals) might be involved in the schooling process and how these people work together.
3. Education as a Specialist Field	*Content* to be mastered and competently applied.	·An exclusive body of evidence-based knowledge for teachers. ·Constitutes what is to be learnt and demonstrated in the teacher education program.
4. Teachers as Researchers		·A focus on expanding the education knowledge base and how teachers approach a constantly changing work context. This is about using research approaches to advance their professional prowess. It encompasses positioning the teacher construct as a catalyst for change in what it means to be schooled and for how young people engage with and prosper in modern society. From an aspirational sense it encompasses how society grows to be a more positive environment for all. This element invokes inquiry, data and analysis, innovation, and entrepreneurship.
5. Teacher Agency		·Positioning the teacher construct in terms of professional competency, professional decision-making, and the required mindsets and confidence levels to take charge of their professional circumstance and to influence others who impact their abilities to practise education.
6. Codified Teaching	A model for how teaching content knowledge is translated into effective practice.	• Formalised and agreed sets of professional procedures and techniques are articulated through standards that define and exemplify "accepted" professional practice.
7. A Theory to Practice Mechanism	The delivery model	• A sustainable model that logically and sustainably captures the component ideas herein with the objective of sequentially scaffolding the transition of the student teacher from novice to effective teaching professional.

The problematic nature of teacher education

At the time of writing, Australian teacher education had undergone yet another teacher education review. In contrast, in England, a new era in teacher education is being ushered in through significant revisions to regulation, policy, and service provision. The United States is a history lesson in ongoing teacher education reform over the past 100 years. The ongoing nature of reviews calls for a rethink of teacher education, and a merry-go-round of government reports point to a field that appears to have lost its way – this is not a recent phenomenon. Researchers such as Tom (1997) 40 or so years ago cited four common criticisms of teacher education programs throughout the Western world, which we argue are still relevant today. His criticisms are that teacher education is vapid, impractical, segmented, and directionless. Specifically, he contends that courses are often superficial and fail to embody the practical knowledge and skills needed by beginning teachers, tending instead to cover pedagogical material that could be better learnt in an apprentice situation. Further, courses developed in universities and other colleges of teacher education tend to have little relationship to each other, often because they have been developed and delivered in separate schools or areas within an education faculty and delivered by specialists in equal isolation. In Australia, in 2000, Richard Smith (2000), a prominent teacher education researcher of the time, signalled emerging social change and the urgent need for fundamental teacher education reform, arguing that myriad attempts at changing teacher education had only deluded teacher educators into thinking that criticisms of teacher education have been countered and that the future is secured. History tells us that the same debates have raged in the 20 years since his writing.

For initial teacher education programs, such as those in England, where school-based models now dominate the preparation logic and where universities are increasingly being left out, we wonder whether student teachers are essentially being encouraged to replicate current practices without the deep specialist knowledge that successful teaching requires. We suspect this model's theory/ practice ingredients might not be calibrated correctly. We say "might" because, at the time of writing, no evaluation was available, nor was it planned. Yet another concern with teacher education is that there are too many gaps in the literature about what works in teacher education. Our concern in all this is that much of the content of present-day teacher education coursework is aligned to "knee-jerk" government policy edicts and the research interests of university academics, as promotion is tied to the necessity to "publish". The conventional teacher education model has largely managed to avoid accountability for specific developmental sequences and particular kinds of course–school linkages, except at a global program level. While we acknowledge there have been pockets of innovation and some radical attempts to rethink teacher education, the reality is that the predominant model of on-campus work, with a somewhat disconnected practicum, still predominates teacher education program thinking. As we said earlier, learning the specifics of how to teach appears to be relegated to when the student teacher enters the workforce. For obvious reasons, this is not acceptable.

Recently, in England and Australia, governments have introduced Core Content Frameworks to focus teacher education providers on what expert panels recommend for initial teacher education. In effect, the state has usurped the agency universities and colleges have had in teacher education design and delivery. Our central concern is that no child, parent, school head, or teacher should be put in the situation of having to cover for an incompetent graduate (or practising teacher) who has been signed off from a teacher education program and accredited by a government or a professional regulator. We further think graduation should be based on proven capacities to teach, not by an amalgam of successful academic assignments, nor by time spent in classrooms, but by student teachers practising the theories as presented and coached and mentored to expert level and, importantly, providing evidence of such effectiveness through their pupils' learning. Any reform must be accompanied by an evaluation for corrective or confirming actions.

The principle of "no excuses" at all levels thus applies so that teacher "quality" is the defining feature when it comes to educational reform, where quality is defined as the capability of a graduate teacher to deliver effective instruction. While practical experience involving a presentation, inference, interpretation, and a pre-theoretical view of teaching is part of the preparation equation, we take the view that the model required for preparing the teacher today is essentially a set of knowledge and skills based on an evidence-based set of concepts operationalised in intentional and focused behaviours and mindsets involving pupils in classrooms. Drawing on the work of Berry (2014), Berry et al. (2013), Lynch (2012), and Smith (2000), we have identified the hallmarks of a teacher preparation logic and regime that supports our thesis of preparing a different type of teacher for a different type of schooling experience, and which is fit for the fundamentally different societal circumstance which young people are growing up in today.

Our central premise is that a transformed teacher education program is positioned through a set of stratified teaching appointments organised through a quadrivial of (i) client-focused curriculum design, (ii) using learning diagnostics as the trigger point for instructions and thus (iii) applying the appropriate pedagogical approach and then conducting (iv) learning and program evaluations, which are undertaken strategically to ascertain learning outcome successes, at an expert level. Above all, teachers will have demonstrated competence to graduate and start teaching work, albeit supported by a consultant, which is a significant distinction in our rethought teacher education program logic. We explore these ideas in greater detail in Chapter 12.

Towards a transformative teacher education model

In this section and Chapter 12, we distil our previous chapter comments and bring together critical points as outlined in Table 11.1 to sketch a preparation program for our new teacher types working in the context of a new grammar of schooling. We begin by making clear our position on teacher education. Does rethinking teacher education mean displacing those perhaps interesting and mind-challenging – but not specific to education – academic and scholarly study subjects commonly found in teaching degree programs? Our response is, "Yes, it does". We contend that, in general, the subjects that fill the programs of teacher education courses and regulatory requirements today cannot make meaningful connections with learning to teach and achieving those desired levels of teaching competency. We believe these areas of knowledge are better placed in other university departments where they may be taken up as electives by teaching candidates or offered as a subject in an initial degree for a later graduate teaching qualification to be built upon. Further, our teacher education program logic would focus on learning key things deeply, not many things superficially. By this, we seek to declutter the current teacher education program. Do we envision students joining the teaching workforce through a cursory preparation regime as "apprentices?" No, we do not. We seek to balance the theory/practice and flesh out what each side of the teacher education ledger needs to focus on. So, let us get started.

First steps in transforming teacher education: A new set of design principles

The first step in rethinking teacher education is to establish a set of design principles. These principles capture key transformative points made earlier in this book and play two key roles in the teacher education design process. First, they focus the teacher educator's mind on the underpinning premise of the required changes and, in effect, make the program distinctive to the current regime. This eliminates the tendency to replicate the past, which has been characteristic of teacher education thinking over many decades. Second, they guide actual program developments by stipulating what needs to be considered as a set of transformative goals to be achieved. We expand on these principles in Chapter 12 as a blueprint for a new teacher education model where we move from theoretical considerations to practical ones. We now outline our five design principles.

Principle 1: Transformative and disruptive

The post-2020 era is characterised by ongoing exponential technology-based change that is redefining work and home life such that what results is a radical departure from the past. Schools, and by direct association, the work of teachers, prepare young people for work and life in such a circumstance. If the world has changed, then schools and teaching must change accordingly. But this new world does not follow the mores of the past: disruption is the modus operandi, where technology is a fundamental element. So, when we speak of change, we take a proactive stance and thus position teacher education as a mechanism that enables teachers to be central in transforming the education system for positive societal outcomes. This neither involves employing ideological warfare nor protest but is about providing quality teaching and learning services that benefit all students. One could call this type of thinking as having a "futures orientation". With this principle, we make clear that teacher education is no longer a university or college challenge but an industry-wide responsibility.

Principle 2: Evidence informed and practice by code

Effective professional education practice is governed by defined and agreed codes of practice. These practice codes take their reference from an evidence base that provides specificity and instructive guidance on how teaching work is undertaken. In turn, the practice codes define what is teacher work and what is not, but importantly articulate a consensus on how teaching work is undertaken, with a near guarantee of success. In simple terms, they professionalise the teaching workforce. Teaching work under such a principle is highly clinical and enmeshed in a set of defined practice codes that easily distinguish the novice or amateur from the professional. In turn, these codes of practice provide a framework for the teacher education program curriculum – a set of goals to be achieved in each student teacher – and, accordingly, the focus for assessment tasks and the criteria for graduation. Practising outside of the codes is malpractice and accordingly the codes define what professional teaching work is and is not.

Principle 3: Bridging the gap between theory and practice

A significant challenge in professional preparation programs is the theory–practice divide. This divide occurs when there is a misfit or misalignment between the goals of the preparation program and the realities of the world where graduates are to be employed. It occurs in a confluence of conflicting ideas, different operational logics, and decisions made in isolation. Mechanisms like collaborative preparation partnerships, where each participant offers distinct yet equitable contributions while aligning on shared objectives, and operational tools such as learning tasks centred on real-world application in authentic contexts with mutual advantages are pivotal foundations for bridging the gap between theory and practice.

Principle 4: From illumination to performativity

Traditional higher education programming, in which most teacher education programs reside, rely on students' illuminating theories and propositions for professional practice using essays, oral presentations, and the like. While a strategy for eliciting understanding, this type of learning approach does not guarantee a personal capacity to do so in the real world. A device is required that enables theory to be honed and practised in the real world as a mechanism for learning how to teach. Taking reference from the other principles, this type of mechanism will be strictly focused and informed by codes of practice, be of mutual benefit to all involved, and thus enmeshed in real-world tasks and objectives while seeking to prepare the teacher for the transformational work that is teaching in a 2000s era context.

Principle 5: Embracing third-space thinking

The idea of a third space emerged from the work of Soja (1996, p. 5), who argued it was "a space of extraordinary openness, a place of critical exchange". The premise of a third space in teacher education is essentially a merging of the operating logic of the university or college (as the teacher education provider) and the school (as the place of teaching work) through a working relationship that seeks alignment in focus towards a mutually agreed agenda. In our case, it is the preparation of teachers and the advancement of the teaching profession more generally. It presupposes that each party will have an equal yet different contribution to be made. However, primarily, it represents a joining of forces and a transformation of how each thinks about and does business to create a more effective and attuned teaching system. This type of arrangement can be understood as a community of practice that expands its focus to include collaborative planning and the sharing of resources and blurring of boundaries between researchers (university) and teachers (school) through engagement in teaching-centric applied research. In summation, third-space thinking takes the locus of authority away from the university or college in the teacher education program. It projects it into a collaboration where agency is agreed and engaged commensurate to respective capabilities and capacities. We reiterate the vital role that these design principles play in teacher education reform. We contend that without reference to such principles, any revision of any teacher education program will recreate the past. Our key point is that a new socio-technical world needs a new set of organisational references. Chapter 12 applies these principles to a set of programming components that bring to life a teacher education program commensurate to a post-2020 era.

The teaching transformation agenda that is forming

- A comprehensive agenda for transforming teaching that emphasises a shift towards futures-oriented, evidence-based, and client-centric approaches to education.
- It proposes seven key elements for teacher education program design, including redefining teacher roles, emphasising specialist knowledge, and promoting teacher agency.
- Advocates for a transformative model that bridges the gap between theory and practice while embracing innovation and disruption.
- Five design principles are proposed to guide the transformation of teacher education, focusing on transformative and disruptive thinking, evidence-informed practice, bridging the theory–practice gap, performativity, and embracing third-space thinking.

References

Berry, B. (2014). Going to scale with teacherpreneurs. *Phi Delta Kappan*, 95(7), 8–14. https://doi.org/10.1177/003172171409500703

Berry, B., Byrd, A., & Wieder, A. (2013). *Teacherpreneurs: Innovative teachers who lead but don't leave*. Wiley.

Hattie, J. (2016). *Shifting away from distractions to improve Australia's schools: Time for a reboot.* https://education.unimelb.edu.au/news-and-events/events/2016/dls/shifting-a way-from-distractions-to-improve-australias-schools

Lynch, D. (2012). *Preparing teachers in times of change: Teaching schools, standards, new content and evidence.* https://doi.org/10.53333/PRHPG/280209

Pearson, N. (2006). *Layered identities and peace.* https://parlinfo.aph.gov.au/parlInfo/sea rch/display/display.w3p;query=Id:%22media/pressrel/MPDK6%22

Smith, R. (2000). The future of teacher education: Principles and prospects. *Asia-Pacific Journal of Teacher Education, 28*(1), 7–28. https://doi.org/10.1080/135986600109417

Soja, E. W. (1996). *Thirdspace: Journeys to Los Angeles and other real-and-imagined places.* Wiley-Blackwell.

Tom, A. R. (1997). *Redesigning teacher education.* Suny Press.

12 A transformational teacher education program

What's our key message?

- A transformational model for teacher education is required to kick start a transformation in teaching, schooling, and education, emphasising the importance of preparing teachers for new schooling experiences.
- Five interrelated mechanisms as practical solutions for implementing teacher education programs are new pathways, teaching schools, portal tasks, new content, and a model for learning how to teach.
- Stratification of teaching work involving different teaching roles prepared through distinct teacher education pathways.
- The concept of a teaching school, akin to a teaching hospital in medicine as a strategic partnership between schools and universities. It focuses on knowledge production and its transmission through practical experience, which serve as central learning and assessment structures.

In Chapter 11, seven elements of teacher education programs and five principles for designing teacher education programs were introduced. These elements and principles work together to capture the multitude of discussions in this book, generating a set of references for designing teacher education (the principles) and accordingly identifying what needs to be factored in (the elements) when the goal is to prepare a different type of teacher for a different type of schooling experience. Missing in our discussions are mechanisms that cause the required changes to occur. In this chapter, we rethink teacher education programming by bringing these elements and principles to life as a set of required mechanisms. These mechanisms emerge as a synthesis of the positions and propositions outlined in this book and as products of our collective work in teacher education research and program development over the past decades. So, we now move our theoretical discussions to the practical by introducing a set of five interrelated mechanisms that give the teacher education program the capacity to prepare a different type of teacher for work in a new grammar of schooling. In simpler terms, we sketch the operational side of teacher education programming to create a set of mechanisms for implementing teacher education. These mechanisms are (i) new teacher education

DOI: 10.4324/9781003303312-15

pathways, (ii) teaching schools as the place for learning to teach and for furthering the evidence base of the profession, (iii) portal tasks as the focus for what needs to be learnt and demonstrated for graduation, (iv) new content required to be learnt, and (v) a model for learning how to teach. We have compiled these five mechanisms into Table 12.1, which references the critical elements discussed in Chapter 11.

New teacher education pathways

In Chapter 8, a stratified teaching workforce was introduced as the centrepiece for teaching work in a new grammar of schooling. Stratification can be understood as a variety of different types and "levels" of teachers – new teaching roles – working collaboratively in schools and co-opting and utilising various paraprofessional roles for specific education outcomes. The goal of stratification is to increase the global capacities of the school to deal with students as individuals in a rethought system of education and to create clarity on school-based roles. It is thus a client-centric model of schooling. In such a model, the classroom teacher is not expected to be all things to all students. Accordingly, the teaching of individuals now expands to a stratified set of teaching roles and those roles are prepared accordingly. With these points in mind and reflecting on our vision for a new era school in Chapters 9 and 10, we envision a continuum of teacher education programs married to the teaching roles in schools. These roles have precursor preparation programs for learning how to teach in an employment context, positioning them for real-life learning work within the schooling system. Table 12.2 defines the scope of teaching applicable to each role.

Table 12.1 Key teacher education elements and principles mapped to key teacher education mechanisms (based on works by David Lynch).

Principle 1: Transformative and Disruptive
Principle 2: Evidence Informed and Practised by Code
Principle 3: Bridging the Gap Between Theory and Practice
Principle 4: From Illumination to Performativity
Principle 5: Embracing Third-Space Thinking

Mechanisms Key elements	New teacher education pathways	Teaching school	Portal tasks	New content	A model for learning how to teach
Stratification of teaching work	X	X	X		
A scope of practice	X	X	X	X	
Teachers as researchers	X	X	X	X	X
Education as a specialist field		X	X	X	
Teacher agency	X	X	X		
Codified teaching		X	X	X	
A theory to practice mechanism		X	X		

Table 12.2 Three teaching roles and their associated teacher education pathways (based on works by David Lynch).

Qualification	Training role	Study focus	Graduating role	Scope of practice
Graduate Diploma	ITE student	• Introduction to the field of education • How to teach and assess student learning	Associate Teacher	Implement and assess a teaching plan for a specific client/client group under the direction of a registered teacher.
Masters	Intern	• How to design an effective teaching plan • How to deliver an effective teaching plan • How to evaluate a teaching plan • Engineering education logistics for learning outcome effects	Registered Teacher	Design, implement, and assess global teaching plans for a specific client/client group and supervise associate teachers and paraprofessionals for individual client outcomes.
Fellowship	Pedagogical Registrar	• How to diagnose learning and strategise complex learning syndromes and circumstances • Whole-school data monitoring and evaluations • Specialist teaching and learning knowledge and skills • Educational research capacities • Coordinators paraprofessional for global student learning and wellbeing outcomes	Consultant	Provide specialist teaching services. Design, deliver, and assess teacher education programming. Conduct and publish educational research. Working with and managing paraprofessionals for learning and wellbeing outcome effects.

Note: ITE = Initial Teacher Education

Recall from Chapter 7 that we proposed three positions-based teaching pathways: associate teacher, registered teacher, and consultant. Teacher education in our model thus begins with applicants entering as initial teacher education (ITE) students and holding a relevant first degree or certified content knowledge specific to an area of teaching. This could include, for example, a trade qualification for those, say, teaching manual arts. This "first-degree" status places a premium on teaching students having expert-level teaching content knowledge on entry and, with it, we signal teacher education as a graduate program. The first level of teacher education for a teaching student would be a graduate diploma teaching qualification that would prepare them for the "associate teacher" role. The associate teacher position represents formal preparation for what was the ubiquitous and traditional teacher aide position, but now the first rung in our stratified teaching regime, as a recognition of how undergraduate teachers should be introduced to and prepared for teaching, but also how skilled staff are now fundamental in teaching-related positions. Small group and individual tutoring under registered teacher supervision has long been a model for dealing with individuals in schools, especially those requiring additional support. The problem with such a traditional aide model is that it is often the most complex cases handed to these unqualified personnel. The evidence clearly shows that the increased funding of these positions in schools has not resulted in improved student outcomes.

In our model, the ITE student begins work in an assigned and accredited place of teacher education, what we term a teaching school, and has a series of "learn to teach" or portal tasks to work on and which act as the assessment centre. These teaching school arrangements invoke our third-space thinking principle. Teacher education is an "agreed arrangement" with schools – as places of teaching work – for specific learning to teach effects. In such an arrangement, ITE students complete a course of study embedded within the business of school and classroom work. This course of study comprises portal task-based teaching assignments supported by a corresponding set of underpinnings delivered and facilitated by consultants. Typical portal task assignments would centre on individual and small group work assignments, cohort learning segments, student safety and wellbeing, and a general introduction to the schooling system. Associate teachers can continue in such roles on graduation or opt for further higher-level study, where they enter as teaching interns and work to graduate as registered teachers.

The registered teacher program, which occurs as a Master of Teaching, extends the associate teacher role by emphasising higher-level expert teaching knowledge and skills, focused on building competency with teaching. In such a preparation program, interns work on various higher-level teaching assignments with the registered teacher as a co-teacher. Accordingly, the emphasis is on the global design, delivery, assessment, and reporting of learning plans for assigned clients. While the registered teacher program is indicatively four years of formal teacher education study – including associate teacher education – the defining feature is studying and learning to apply expert-level education knowledge. This happens in the context of close coaching and mentoring. The candidate can graduate only by demonstrating that they can teach, judged with evidence of student learning and a series of peer reviews. Once again, a formal study program supports and underpins this preparation regime and is a vital role of the consultant.

The final level of teacher education is that of the "teaching registrar", which prepares registered teachers for work as consultants. As Chapter 7 revealed, the consultant is the pinnacle of the career move in the teaching profession. The consultant role is the medical equivalent of the "specialist", not just from a teaching content area perspective but also with regard to pedagogical prowess. The consultant acts within a regime of professional referrals, consultations, and specialist-level education service provisions and strategically orchestrates teaching teams for overall schooling effects. The program of study prepares the consultant to conduct learning diagnostics and develop specialist needs-based plans and interventions, enact whole-of-school or whole-of-system evaluations, conduct research in the education field, and act as knowledge custodians and facilitators in the teacher education program. Globally, the consultant represents the professional leadership of education in our schools and other places of learning. This preparation program takes the form of a teaching registrar, and graduation to consultant is commensurate to gaining a fellowship in an esteemed college of medicine. This college, a parallel to medical colleges, transitions the system of higher education from a confluence of disparately connected university education faculties, academic journals, and professional associations into a sophisticated professional body that curates, expands, packages, and evaluates the field of education and the programming of teacher education. It is the peak professional body for educators. We believe that creating the role of consultants and the meeting of such great minds forms the establishment of an esteemed college. Formalising the college is one step towards addressing the arguments of ministers of education and policymakers when they seek greater esteem for those who teach and the return of teacher agency to the business of education. This esteemed college logic is a theme we explore in Chapter 13, where we discuss transitionary arrangements.

The teaching school

Invoking third-space thinking, the teaching school is parallel to the "teaching hospital" in medicine, where the collective capacities and endeavours of a school (Kindergarten to 12) and a university (in this case, an education faculty) are harnessed through formal partnership to constitute the operations of the teacher education program. What traditionally was "schoolwork" and that which was "university work" in teacher education are combined such that each "partner" has an equal yet different contribution to be made in the improving teaching and learning agenda. There are no traditional organisational boundaries, but each partner has a unique key role based on their expertise and charter. If one envisions the school and the university (through its education faculty) joining forces to focus on knowledge production and its transmission as a multi-purpose and multi-dimensional entity, where each party has an equal yet different contribution to make, the following logics prevail:

- When one is working in the school, one is also working in the university (and vice versa).
- Staff in the school thus teach in the school and in the university.
- When staff in the school "work", they also research and engage in professional learning.
- When staff in the school research and learn, they also acquire credentials and qualifications and contribute to the research base as researchers and knowledge producers.
- When staff in the school teach their students, they join forces with the university to evaluate outcomes, solve problems, test propositions for improvement, and work to achieve quality educational outcomes for students.
- When school staff, teacher education students, and the university work together, they significantly increase the capacity and capability of each organisation.

The teaching school is thus a strategic partnership between a school and a university to prepare future teachers and represents a radical rethink of how teacher education research is undertaken. To focus the teaching school on the business of teacher education and to generate mutually beneficial outcomes, portal tasks are enacted as the central structure through which the process of learning to teach is enacted and the assessment of teaching abilities is decided.

Portal tasks

Portal tasks are the conceptual and practical mechanism through which theory is connected to practice and content to demonstrable student learning outcomes employing creative tasks and an assessment regime. Portal tasks are undertaken only in teaching schools, which are regular schools or training institutions. A portal task is defined for ITE students as a "learn-by-doing task", and each is framed as learning to teach in a given curriculum circumstance (for example, the teaching of reading, physical education, or mathematics). Portal tasks have four distinct and interlinked foci. First, they define the curriculum for the teaching school. Each portal task embodies and represents sets of codified practices to be practised and achieved and, by association, the specialist education knowledge to be learnt while the teaching student is in a teaching school. These assigned practice codes define success attributes for associated learning and assessment purposes. Second, portal tasks articulate specific developmental skills that the teacher education student must concentrate on during their time in their teaching school. Thus, portal tasks are highly clinical in that they focus on learning how to teach in an intensive and focused fashion. Third, each portal task acts as a defined teaching/learning task that broadly engages the teaching student in "designing and delivering learning experiences". In all cases, the portal task is flexible to fit the school and classroom context. It is developed, implemented, and evaluated in a context of what can be termed a learner-mediated partnership – a focus on what the ITE student needs to learn and achieve – with an assigned coach and mentor. Fourth, portal tasks are engineered in the context of the student and their assigned "learn-to-teach mentor" working as researchers. To "pass" a portal task, the ITE student must demonstrate, with the support of evidence, that they have achieved the defined teaching standards assigned to each portal task with their client/ client group and within a defined learning context. The sum of achievement in each portal task across the program represents graduation readiness.

The teaching school and portal task mechanisms are key to our model's thinking in forming the specific and clinical "learning to teach" part of the program. To appreciate how teaching schools and portal tasks impact the overall teacher education program, one has to appreciate that at the heart is a student of a teaching-centric community of practice (CoP), known as a "learner-mediated partnership" (Stephenson, 1999). This learning arrangement is designed to increase the ITE student's teaching proficiencies and the host school's teaching and organisational capabilities.

New content

With Principle 1 (transformative and disruptive) in mind, the focus of our teacher education program is clearly on preparing the teacher to teach the curriculum and for each student to succeed. These foci are disruptive to the tradition of teacher work because they cause the school to rethink its required workforce to include a cadre of "paraprofessionals" to generate a movement from mass education to client-centric arrangements. Our new teacher construct is thus not everything to everyone. By direct association, our new schooling construct is set up to be potentially everything the individual student requires. The preparation of paraprofessionals such as speech therapists, occupational therapists, and the like is the purview of their respective professions, so they do not figure in our preparation model.

Returning to the focus on learning how to teach, one must consider the context in which young people now attend school. Modern-day schooling occurs in the context of ongoing exponential technology-based changes. These changes are redefining home and work life, disrupting all aspects of society, and rendering the society of just 30 years ago truly prehistoric by comparison. Think artificial intelligence, automation, and robots, which are converging into yet more sophisticated technologies, causing society to think about what roles human beings might have in the coming decades. Schools prepare people for future life, so teacher education must position teachers to work for such a future, not as "another" player, but as a key agent in a society now built on knowledge and its exploitation for the new and novel. On a parallel and directly related plane, we are witnessing a societal revolution where the wellbeing, safety, and inclusion of young people with various profiles are now foremost in society's minds. This is now the preparation context.

Our new model for teacher education thus represents a signing off from the past and the repositioning of the teacher as a key knowledge worker, where young people are prepared for work and life in the post-2020 era. The program we envision is thus viewed as being disruptive to the traditional notions of "education" and "schooling" in that it aims to transform the role of teachers and position them squarely in the "what does it mean to be educated" space. In such programming, a premium is placed on learning how to teach. However, this premium is embedded in a realisation that society is in flux and, with it, new knowledge and skills are required to effect a new approach to teaching in such a context. We term this sense of disruption through designing and effectively delivering programs for learning for "the future" a futures orientation. The knowledge and skills informing a futures orientation were outlined in Chapter 8 in Table 8.1.

A futures orientation can be understood as a set of complementary knowledge and skills and a corresponding mindset that views the future as something that can be shaped and exploited for positive outcomes. Such an orientation means having a personal capacity to interpret and plan for future circumstances and effect positive change. Futures orientation is, therefore, a capability that enables an individual to envision possibilities that lie ahead, make corresponding plans, evaluate such plans, define how those plans can be implemented, and identify likely consequences or outcomes of such plans. This is in contrast to traditional teaching mindsets, where tinkering means being in a constant state of catch-up. Future concepts and the discourses they support provide the education field with the resources for planning, social innovation, and the creation of new ways of doing and responding. This notion contributes to people's empowerment in determining their futures. It provides insight into what may eventually happen, reducing the degree of uncertainty characteristic of a fast-evolving Knowledge Society, as explained in Chapters 1 to 3.

In summary, our new teacher education program is highly focused on learning how to teach. However, it is oriented to position teacher work, schooling, and education more broadly as a futures-oriented pursuit. There will be a role gap in such an approach to teaching work, and this is where our new teacher construct departs the "be everything to everyone" logic because a variety of paraprofessionals who have the necessary expertise to deal with non-teaching-related things enter the schooling workforce as a member of a multi-disciplinary team.

With Principle 2 (evidence informed and practice by code) in mind and reflecting on points made in previous chapters about what needs to change in teaching, schooling, and teacher education, five key study areas emerge as indicators of the things to be learnt in our new teacher education program. These areas would be presented commensurate to graduation roles (for associate teacher, registered teacher, and consultant) and include (i) the study of education as a specialist field, (ii) teaching content knowledge, (iii) technology, (iv) futures-orientation studies, and (v) teaching and learning systems. We do not propose to provide a detailed outline of the related content here, as curating it for teacher education effects is a transitionary consideration that we take up in Chapter 13. The study areas are thus outlined to illustrate the programming focus for the required teacher education program, as mentioned in the previous section. We use Table 12.3 to illustrate these five study areas and the associated foci.

Table 12.3 Five study areas for teacher education programming (based on works by David Lynch).

Study area	Goals for teaching graduates	Indicative content
Education	• A capacity to diagnose, design, implement, and assess a teaching program for various learner profiles. • A capacity to engage with and implement codified practice. • A capacity to evaluate a teaching program to ascertain outcomes and remedial effects.	• The science of learning • Learning disabilities • Learning diagnostics • Education theory • Pedagogy • Codified practice • Curriculum design • Program evaluation
Teaching Content Knowledge	• Knowledge competency with required teaching content areas.	• Curriculum area content knowledge • Content knowledge hierarchies
Technology	• A capacity to design, apply/exploit, and evaluate a variety of technological mediums and platforms for learning outcome effects.	• Technology competencies • Web 2.0 technologies • Disruptive technologies
Futures	• A knowledge base, mindset, and a set of specific strategic creatives that enable the positioning of learning designs for future circumstances.	• Futures studies • Mindsets for innovation and creativity • Strategic planning
Teaching and Learning Systems	• A capacity to conceptualise, operate within, and innovate on circumstances and systems for specific teaching and learning outcome effects. • A capacity to work with paraprofessionals to optimise learning outcomes.	• Schooling • Client centred models/programming • Working with paraprofessionals • Blended learning

A model for learning how to teach

The biggest impediment to our proposed teacher education rethink is the availability of a curated body of expert teaching knowledge packaged for teacher education effects. The education profession has not yet reached a level of maturity where teaching practice has been codified. Thus, a consensus has not been achieved on what teachers need to know and how associated practice is undertaken. It is fair to say that current teacher education programming is presented as a smorgasbord of education theories, ideas, and mandated knowledge requirements (cultural competencies, child safety, and the like), the content of which is primarily determined by the research interests of the associated teacher educator. It is left to the ITE student to locate all this into their practice when they graduate as a teacher.

We propose two key mechanisms to effect a learn-to-teach logic in teacher education. The first is a set of interrelated teaching planning scaffolds. These scaffolds capture and organise key teaching requirements into the teacher education curriculum, guiding the ITE students as they plan and deliver their teaching plans. The second is a coaching and mentoring arrangement that focuses the ITE student on learning how to teach in a real-life teaching situation. The scope and intensity of each mechanism reflect the teacher's preparation level. To give substance to our logic, we will focus on ITE, a critical area of concern. Preparation at the consultant level would follow a similar logic but have a greater sense of sophistication and be heavily research concentric. We turn first to teaching planning scaffolds.

Two interrelated teaching planning scaffolds

From our experience in teacher education, curriculum organisers such as the "Learning Management Design Process" and "Dimensions of Learning" are illustrative of the type of content organiser we think effective undergraduate teacher education programming requires. We acknowledge there are others, but we have chosen these two as they align with the research evidence we present regarding them in Chapter 13. We briefly discuss each to illustrate their scope and logic. The Learning Management Design Process, also known as "the Eight Learning Management Questions", is a teaching planning framework that draws the ITE student to the essential, research-based elements of a successful teaching plan. These eight sequential questions and the Dimensions of Learning research provide a coherent and systematic framework for scaffolding ITE students in how to teach. These questions provide a design sequence that enables teacher education students and an assigned coach and mentor to focus on achieving learning outcomes for their allocated class (their students). Table 12.4 illustrates these questions.

Table 12.4 The learning design process.

LMQ1	What has my student achieved to date?	Outcomes achieved to date
LMQ2	What do I aim to achieve in my student?	Setting focal learning outcomes
LMQ3	How does my student best learn?	Profiling the student and their learning dispositions
LMQ4	What resources do I have at my disposal?	Identification of resources available
LMQ5	What are my teaching strategies?	Dimensions of Learning is consulted for teaching strategies
LMQ6	Who will do what to support my teaching strategies?	Marshalling a team of "others" for teaching outcome effects.
LMQ7	How will I check that my student has achieved the learning outcomes?	Identifying assessments
LMQ8	How will I report student progress	Informing the student and "others" about progress

Correspondingly, the teacher education content is organised and delivered to teaching students in content areas that underpin each question. Simply put, each learning management question is supported by a specific teacher education course or suite of courses, providing the ITE student with a ready reference of knowledge and skills when answering each question. This arrangement is how codified teaching practice is presented and learnt. Dimensions of Learning provides a comprehensive research-based pedagogical model to alert ITE students to the importance of teaching practice in contrast to each of them making up activities: the art and craft logic. When the student comes to the learning management question that asks them to consider their teaching plans, Dimensions of Learning provides a set of evidence-based teaching strategies and their understanding of where they are best used. The point is that if the goal is for all student clients to learn specific things, then creatively making up activities for kids to consume in classrooms is a "hit-and-miss" approach to teaching. While we appreciate that teacher creativity in teaching is essential, as Marzano (2003) and Hattie (2009) argue, creativity alone is insufficient if the approach is devoid of an evidence base showing that it works and, importantly, if the goal is for students to learn specific things. Put another way, creativity without evidence would be considered mal-practice in other professions. This emphasis on pedagogical strategies means that the program instructors must have a good knowledge of pedagogical strategies.

Dimensions of Learning is helpful as it creates a "common language" about teaching. What we mean by this is that each ITE student and their coach and mentors have a common language to explain what they are doing and why – and as a diagnostic tool when "unpacking" the taught lesson to identify "faults" in the teaching approach, thus improving teaching performance. Continuing the Dimensions of Learning theme, this body of work suggests that the following instructional techniques should be used by teachers regardless of the instructional goals that are the focus of a unit of instruction (Marzano, 1998, p. 34). In our model for teacher education, we would adhere to this understanding:

- When presenting new knowledge or processes to students, provide them with advanced ways of thinking about the new knowledge or processes before presenting them.
- When presenting students with new knowledge or processes, help them to identify what they already know about the topic.
- When students have been presented with new knowledge or processes, have them compare and contrast it with other knowledge and processes.
- Help students represent new knowledge and processes in non-linguistic and linguistic ways.
- Have students utilise what they have learnt by engaging them in tasks that involve experimental inquiry, problem-solving, and (presumably) decision-making and investigation.
- Provide students with explicit instructional goals and give them explicit and precise feedback relative to how well those goals were met.

- When students have met an instructional goal, praise and reward their accomplishments.
- Have students identify their instructional goals, develop strategies to obtain them, and monitor their progress and thinking relative to those goals.
- When presenting new knowledge or processes, help students analyse their beliefs that will enhance or inhibit their chances of learning the new knowledge or processes (Smith & Lynch, 2010).

The strong emphasis in Dimensions of Learning on pedagogical strategies that incorporate what is typically called curriculum development is an attractive feature of the approach for teacher educators because learning outcomes are always at the forefront of their work. Strategies for achieving learning cannot be deferred in Dimensions of Learning planning, as in many other teacher education approaches that focus primarily on curriculum or the learner. For these reasons, we argue that the Dimensions of Learning framework is a coherent pedagogical approach to replace the fragmentation and incompleteness of individual lecturers following their predilections and interests.

The teaching transformation agenda that is forming

- A stratified teaching workforce model, emphasising the need for various teaching roles to work collaboratively in schools. Outlining different teaching pathways, starting from an ITE program leading to roles such as associate teacher, registered teacher, and consultant.
- A teaching school as a strategic partnership between schools and universities, akin to a teaching hospital in medicine. It serves as a place for teacher education where theory and practice are integrated.
- Portal tasks act as a practical mechanism that connect theory and practice in teacher education. Portal tasks involve learning-by-doing assignments focused on specific curriculum circumstances and serve as a means to demonstrate teaching proficiency and readiness for graduation.
- A futures-oriented approach to teacher education, preparing teachers to meet the evolving needs of modern schooling with five key study areas for teacher education programming: education as a specialist field, teaching content knowledge, technology, futures-orientation studies, and teaching and learning systems.

References

Hattie, J. (2009). *Visible learning: A synthesis of over 800 meta-analyses relating to achievement.* Routledge. www.taylorfrancis.com/books/mono/10.4324/9780203887332/visible-learning-john-hattie

Marzano, R. J. (1998). What are the general skills of thinking and reasoning and how do you teach them? *The Clearing House*, 71(5), 268–273. https://doi.org/10.1080/00098659809602721

Marzano, R. J. (2003). *What works in schools: Translating research into action*. ASCD.

Smith, R., & Lynch, D. E. (2010). *Rethinking teacher education: Teacher education in a knowledge age*. https://doi.org/10.53333/AACLM/440245

Stephenson, J. (1999). *Corporate capability: Implications for the style and direction of work-based learning*. Research Centre for Vocational Education and Training. www.voced.edu.au/content/ngv:18462

Part 4
Conclusions

13 What's been done before, and what can we learn from it?

> **What's our key message?**
>
> - Existing research emphasises the role of teachers and school leaders in driving educational transformation, highlighting the importance of their knowledge, skills, and decision-making capacities.
> - Initiatives such as the Collaborative Teacher Learning Model (CTLM) showcase successful school-wide improvement programs focused on teamwork and mutual learning among teachers, leading to enhanced student learning outcomes.
> - Challenges in teaching transformation programs include issues of teacher satisfaction, workload, and resistance to change.
> - Studies into teacher education programs reveal the importance of partnerships between schools and universities, emphasising the need for a cohesive approach to preparing teachers for futures-oriented pedagogies.

In this chapter, we seek to understand what has been done before in the teaching transformation space, take stock of the critical things that need to be considered for success, and consider how these inform our teaching transformation ideas. We seek to learn about undertaking transformation in education, teaching and schooling, and teacher education and ensure our proposals have a higher chance of success. Reviewing the educational research literature, one begins to realise that there are plenty of reports on what works in teaching and learning – the component pieces – and the primacy of teacher and school leader work in such outcomes. While teaching and school improvement is well populated, the teaching transformation field, with insights into long-term implementation successes, is scant, with studies tending to focus on some "improvement angle" or specific situations.

Given the centrality of the teacher construct in our book, it is concerning that there are very few large-scale and longitudinal studies into teacher education, especially from the perspective of graduate teachers' capabilities – how well they can teach and their career development post-graduation. Most teacher education

DOI: 10.4324/9781003303312-17

studies are small scale and tend to focus on one aspect of a program or the attitudes of student teachers and their mentors to that program. The lack of deep and insightful research is unhelpful given the vital role that the teacher plays in achieving student learning outcomes and the centrality of their role in our transformational agenda. Despite this circumstance, we have identified a few studies that go some way to understanding what teaching transformation requires and the pitfalls in trying to achieve it. Let us start with teaching and schooling transformation before exploring teacher education.

Schooling transformation

What is evident in the literature is that teachers are crucial players of change in the school improvement process; having the required knowledge, skills, and decision-making capacities are requisite characteristics. Reports such as Wenner and Campbell (2016) and Lin (2014) cite the challenging nature of teaching improvement programs and point to the strategic and enabling role that school leaders play in ensuring optimal and sustained engagement through a change process. We can understand schooling transformation processes as collaborative activities where leaders orchestrate and build teaching talent.

One large-scale study is a five-year research and development program by Lynch (2012) into a school initiative called the Collaborative Teacher Learning Model (CTLM) in Australia. The study investigated a school-wide improvement program that increased student learning outcomes by prioritising teamwork and mutual learning among teachers. The CTLM can be described as an orchestration of leadership, specifically pedagogically based and targeted teacher professional learning, data analysis, and multi-dimensional teamwork. The model encourages sharing insights, methodologies, and effective practices and has its hallmarks in stratifying the teaching workforce for individual student client effects. Teachers in the CTLM reported refined teaching techniques and acknowledged the significant advancements in student learning outcomes. The motivation for the CTLM, aside from wanting to improve students' learning outcomes, was the challenge John Hattie's (2009) *Visible Learning* logic posed. Hattie argued that achieving an effect size in learning outcomes of 0.4, the average impact of factors in his research, or above, was the benchmark, or students were going backwards. It is safe to say that the CTLM model proved it could be achieved and confirmed the required elements of transformation within the school.

Nevertheless, there is another side to this school and the CTLM, which is informative in understanding teaching transformation programs. First, it is crucial to appreciate that before the CTLM started, teacher satisfaction was at an all-time high. The school leader was popular, and teacher retention was high. Fast forward to the end of the study period, and the opposite was true. Teachers cited increased workload and a reduction in what they thought was their right to teaching autonomy. This reflected the highly focused nature of the CTLM, with teachers receiving regular feedback on performance with highly instructive advice on what they should be doing and how. The school leader left the school shortly after the study concluded. Despite both physical and pedagogical innovations in place, the incoming principal, who had many years in a similar role, decided at his first all-staff meeting to cease the CTLM and allow teachers to do what they thought best for their assigned cohort. As one teacher recalls, he said, "You have all worked extremely hard over the past five years, and it is now time to bring back the fun". The national testing scores for this school plummeted in the following year, and despite this, the CTLM has not made a comeback. However, some elements of the CTLM, such as data analysis and teamwork, were reinstated, and the previous principal's legacy has been largely diluted.

The narrative in this chapter delves deeply into the cultural hurdles encountered during the school's transformation process. Earlier chapters shed light on the socio-cultural norms that have influenced teachers and their practices, exemplified by this case. Moreover, it underscores the significant influence of school leadership and educational oversight in permitting such setbacks. Additionally, it underscores the issue of teacher workload; despite recognising the successes of the CTLMs, teachers did not perceive them as a sustainable means to achieve job satisfaction and maintain a healthy work–life balance.

Looking further into the teaching improvement landscape, we can reference the Gates Teacher Effectiveness Program (Stecher et al., 2018). The multi-million-dollar ($575m) program focused on making teachers more effective. In the program, teachers were engaged in designing teacher evaluation systems and then engaged in remedial/responsive professional learning programs. New career pathways were developed, and bonuses were applied for high performance. Despite the significant investment and the involvement of teachers, the initiative did not achieve its goals for student achievement or graduation. The report's recommendations speak to the challenges of changing teaching.

- Reformers should not underestimate the resistance that could arise if changes to teacher evaluation systems have significant negative consequences for staff employment.
- A near-exclusive focus on teacher education might be insufficient to improve student outcomes dramatically. Many other factors might need to be addressed: early childhood education, students' social and emotional competencies, the school learning environment, and family support. Dramatic improvement in outcomes will likely require attention to many of these factors.
- It is crucial to assess the implementation of each new policy and procedure to comprehend how the distinct components of the reform impact outcomes.

Programs such as the CTLM and the Gates Teacher Effectiveness Program tell us that transforming teaching in schools is challenging, with the Gates initiative indicating that extensive funding regimes are not silver bullets. This is not a comment that it cannot be done, but a realisation that leadership is central, that teachers make or break school change programs, and that the educational research landscape is not robust enough to provide the required and informed instructive guidance.

Teacher education research

As we indicated in our introduction, there are very few large-scale studies into teacher education. Those published tend to focus on attitudes rather than examining teaching competence. Despite this, we can reference four studies conducted in the Bachelor of Learning Management (BLM) program established in 2000 at Central Queensland University to gain critical insight into teacher education programming. The BLM is insightful for this book as it was the first significant rethink on teacher education in Australia, which was uniquely subject to actual program research scrutiny. Further, the BLM program mirrors our positions in this book in that it was designed to create a transformation in teaching and teacher education. The program was designed to create a new type of teacher who can work in a circumstance of ongoing socio-technological change and be positioned to effect change in the prevailing education system. Accordingly, the program created teaching schools and portal tasks as innovative mechanisms for practicum and assessment in partnership with the teaching community and codified teaching practice through the use of Dimensions of Learning (Marzano & Pickering, 2006) and the eight Learning Management Questions (Lynch, 2012). The program engineered these elements to apply a "futures orientation". This orientation was defined as a personal capacity to work in current schooling contexts (workplace ready) and having knowledge and skills to effect change in the schooling system commensurate to ongoing socio-technological change.

The first study is a lead BLM-focused study conducted by Lynch (2012), where graduates of the BLM were compared with those graduating from the previous Bachelor of Education (BEd) program. His research identified three crucial insights. First, graduate student capabilities were enhanced when the intervening variables of learning to be workplace ready, program delivered as a partnership with schools, and a futures orientation operated in a teacher preparation program. Second, regarding the perception of students and mentors, the BLM program contributed more to the capabilities of graduates than the BEd program. Third, graduate student mentors implement teacher-centred (or traditional) classroom activities when student teachers are present. This restricts the scope graduate students have to experience and explore "futures-orientation" capabilities in schools and may inadvertently reinforce the student teacher view that a futures orientation has little or no place in the classroom. However, this finding was not consistent at one Central Queensland University (CQU) campus, where mentors were involved in the development and delivery of the BLM program. Here, they reported insights into the BLM program consistent with the program's futures-oriented intent, indicating they had knowledge of the concept and could speak to the program's objectives. This speaks volumes about the need for co-design with the teaching profession.

Overall, however, an analysis of BLM and BEd data by Lynch (2012) found that the BLM course and its delivery modes emerged as the preferred mode of teacher preparation by both student teachers and their in-school mentors. His findings confirm the apparent inadequacies of traditional teacher education programs, as identified in previous chapters of this book. Of interest was how unfamiliar many in-school mentors were with the content of the BLM. Lynch (2012, p. 165) argued that "developing a futures orientation must be accomplished in all teachers who mentor student teachers if teaching students are to benefit … in all facets of the program". It appears that relying on existing traditionally trained teachers is insufficient for repositioning schools or the education system if a futures orientation is the policy vision. This conclusion places a heavy importance on the theoretical element of partnership and its features. It also reinforces the need for all mentors to be accomplished in that student teachers have to experience and learn in such classrooms, meaning teaching mentors must also be learning what is in the program as part of their involvement in such new programs. In summary, Lynch's (2012) BLM study provides evidence that:

- A teacher education program premised on the contents of what CQU termed "futures oriented pedagogies", which comprise the courses and modes of delivery, emerges as the preferred mode of teacher preparation.
- BLM graduates indicated they were better prepared for the future; in-school mentors reinforced this.
- Workplace readiness is a core variable in a teacher education program if the program aims to graduate teachers who are both "capable" and competent.
- A "futures orientation" affiliated with government and education policy needs to be accomplished rather than assumed in mentors who participate in a teacher education partnership. To be effective, the theoretical element "futures orientation" implies new knowledge to be learnt within a community of practice partnership.
- The concept of a "community of practice" relies on each party's involvement in learning. It is difficult, perhaps impossible in an emerging Knowledge Economy, for any community of practice to remain insulated and current.

Further to Lynch's (2012) BLM study, three further studies have been conducted into the BLM. The first study was conducted by Ingvarson et al. (2005) from the Australian Council for Education Research (ACER) in 2004. The second was a doctoral study by Allen (2009), which investigated the capacity of the BLM to bridge the theory–practice gap, a long-identified problem between the university and the workplace. The third, a doctoral study by Doe (2011), investigated the teaching school partnership idea (i.e. the university working with a school under a set of agreements) that underpinned the BLM and associated teacher professional learning. Drawing on these reports, we discuss each in turn before making further comments on the efficacy of the BLM program.

Ingvarson et al. (2005) were commissioned by the then federal education minister, the Hon. Brendan Nelson, to report the outcomes of the BLM program. While the Lynch (2012) study was focused on one institution (graduates of Central Queensland University), this second study incorporated other universities and had an observed teaching component. Accordingly:

The brief for the [ACER Study by Ingvarson et al., 2005] evaluation was to focus mainly on the outcomes of teacher education, not methods or procedures. In terms of the outcome measures used in this study, the BLM approach is producing graduates who believe that they are better prepared for the first year of teaching than are graduates from other Queensland universities. This belief is supported by observational evidence that showed a sample of BLM graduates taught at a significantly higher standard than a sample of graduates from other Queensland universities. School principals also believed that BLM graduates were better prepared than other graduates.

(Ingvarson et al., 2005, p. 78)

Drawing on the findings of this study and as outlined in Smith and Lynch (2010, pp. 12–27), the following about the BLM can be reported.

Emphasis on training in a core model of effective pedagogy

The BLM program requires university staff and teacher mentors to present students with a basic architecture typical to effective learning management, no matter what is being taught. This architecture is found in the BLM Learning Design Process (Eight Learning Management Questions) and Dimensions of Learning. It provides students with a common framework for designing pedagogical strategies that achieve learning outcomes. The framework prioritises linkages between outcomes, assessment, and pedagogical practice. The program actively promotes a "consistently applied, 'deep structure' model of pedagogy, based on standards for effective teaching, [that] appears to have borne fruit" (Ingvarson et al., 2005, p. 79).

Active engagement in learning how to use the model

In addition to students learning how to handle the core elements of the Design Process and Dimensions of Learning, they are regularly placed in workplace situations from the beginning of their program. Work placements provide the opportunity and responsibility to apply the principles of effective pedagogy as defined in the program. This element of the BLM requires that schoolteachers understand the same model and can mentor and coach students.

Strong linkages between theory and practice

Each course in the BLM operates according to an algorithm of one piece of assessment for the conceptual issues and a second piece for the demonstration of performance in the workplace (the portal task). This assessment regime ensures that all BLM graduate teachers get to know the field and can demonstrate applications of core concepts and procedures in situ. This essential element in the BLM links university subjects to workplace experiences, a gap noted by many educational researchers in the teacher education field. Teacher professional accountability is enhanced in a regime that requires student teachers to demonstrate that they can promote student learning based on expertise.

An authentic partnership between schools, employing authorities, and the university

The partnership concept between stakeholders in which equal but different contributions are recognised and valued lies at the heart of the learning management concept. The teaching school captures and organises this intent.

Standards-based teacher education

According to Ingvarson et al. (2005, p. 97), the BLM program is "a thorough-going example of standards-based teacher education". This means that the criteria for judging the program's success are external to the graduate performances and the program itself. For example, it is instructional theory rather than learning theory oriented.

A third study into the BLM was conducted by Allen (2009), where she compared the logic of the BLM with the effects of university lecturers and school mentors on the teaching practice and beliefs of recent graduates employed in a school system. The study was conducted in the context of one of CQU's five BLM program campuses. Her results indicated several crucial points. First, where there is a weak partnership between schools and the teacher education faculty, the logic of the BLM breaks down and often becomes non-existent. Examples include such things as failure by BLM in-school learning managers (teachers in schools who act as mentors of BLM students) and university staff to establish and nurture relationships with schools and teachers. Presumably, some university staff, principals, and teachers do not see "partnership" as a worthwhile exercise, indicating the resilience of the "us and them" mentality of schools and universities regarding teacher education programs.

Second, as with findings in the study outlined by Lynch (2012), where the logic of the BLM is unknown to or is not sustained by either lecturers or mentor teachers, the logic is undermined and has little effect on the graduate teacher. Here, Allen provided evidence indicating that university staff either ignored the BLM theoretical framework or actively undermined it by substituting content in their teaching. Similarly, teacher mentors required student teachers and later graduates to conform to school practices. For others, there were misunderstandings and often little understanding of BLM concepts and practices despite several years of professional development and learning, especially with university-based staff.

Third, where lecturers and teachers insist on teaching their knowledge components outside the BLM curriculum, such as substituting constructivism and learning theory for instructional theory or requiring student teachers and new graduates to conform to a school practice, the BLM model collapses. Also, Allen's data shows that the school ethos of every teacher doing "their own thing" was shared with university-based staff. There seems to be little appreciation of the

BLM's avowed intention to develop a "consistently applied, "deep structure" model of pedagogy, based on standards for effective teaching in either university teaching or school mentoring. As Smith and Lynch (2010, p. 26) explain:

> there are few rewards in universities for the conduct of programs like the BLM which are heavily "professional" and are time-heavy. Similarly, suppose the BLM model is poorly understood and implemented. In that case, it appears to have a few upsides for schools as the different demands of the BLM are perceived and interpreted in the old "prac" model terms.

The fourth study, by Doe (2011), investigated the premise of professional (teacher) learning through the teaching school concept (conceptually known as the "Professional Learning Project"), where Dimensions of Learning was the learning focus. Dimensions of Learning is key to the BLM "learning to teach model" in that it provides pedagogical guidance in the BLM and contributes to a futures orientation in both BLM students and their in-school classroom teacher mentors. Doe (2011) found that a professional learning partnership with a university can generate professional learning outcomes in teachers, but this is problematic for reasons outlined by Allen (2009). Difficulties arose from leadership, different system priorities, communication systems, competing agendas, and other partnership elements such as "trust". More specifically, Doe (2011) concluded that the differing systems (the teacher education faculty and the school/education system) generate a variety of conflicts. However, she added that if these were adequately dealt with, such initiatives would prosper.

When reviewing the studies by Lynch (2012), Allen (2009), and Doe (2011), what comes to light is that the elements lauded by Ingvarson et al. (2005) are most likely to generate intransigence in teacher education faculties and schools. This co-production of the status quo by self-generating mindsets and interpretive frameworks remains a fundamental reason why it is difficult to change the practices of schools and education faculties. Preparing a different type of teacher must consider these contextual conditions (Smith & Lynch, 2010). The BLM's chief weakness, however, appears to manifest in the different cultures that exist in school and teacher education faculties, which tend to make developing and sustaining a cohesive teacher education partnership between schools and the university, as the teacher education provider, problematic. As Lynch (2012), Allen (2009), and Doe (2011) found, a school + teacher education faculty partnership is a crucial requirement for a re-engineered teacher education program, especially one that has unfamiliar (to current teachers) content to be learnt and practised. Nevertheless, there must also be a mindset in both parties that is committed to actual change if such change is to be genuinely pursued and sustained. This tends to suggest that an arrangement whereby "partners" (i.e. school and teacher education faculty staff) can work together (co-exist/co-locate) and thus develop an appropriate culture for teacher education programming is an advantageous situation. Thus, it can be concluded that all parties must be engaged in learning any new content – not just assuming such capabilities are present in school mentors and teacher educators – and be committed to making such change a priority if this component is to have a chance of success in graduating a different type of teacher.

There is a postscript to these studies: the BLM program was phased out by CQU in 2009, and programming returned to the BEd program. The hallmarks of the BLM have disappeared and are replaced with the standard teacher education lingo and logic. This speaks volumes as to the politics and ideological clashes that play out in teacher education faculties when change is mooted, in that a traditional programming logic appears to resonate more with the reward systems of the education faculty and the ideological priories that they espouse. What is staggering here is that the research evidence pointing to the effectiveness of the BLM was not strong enough, nor was the profession's admiration for the program loud enough, to deter such a roll-back.

While these studies may suggest that changing education, schooling, teaching, and teacher education is a hopeless task, the reality is that these studies provide critical insights into what the work of change requires. Accordingly, these need to be designed into any "transformation" program. In that context, we hope our outline positions our transformation agenda for success. In the following chapter, we close off on this point by outlining our teaching transformation agenda by taking stock of our ideas discussed in this book to prefigure a strategy for the critical next steps.

The teaching transformation agenda that is forming

- The importance of understanding past efforts in teaching transformation, identifying critical success factors, and incorporating these insights into future strategies is paramount.
- The essential role of teachers and school leaders in driving transformational change within schools, emphasising the need for collaborative approaches and strategic leadership.
- There may be challenges and complexities of implementing teaching improvement initiatives.
- A need for innovative approaches that bridge the theory–practice gap, prioritise futures-oriented pedagogies, and foster genuine partnerships between universities and schools.

References

Allen, J. (2009). *The" theory-practice gap": Turning theory into practice in a pre-service teacher education program.* CQUniversity. www.researchgate.net/profile/Jeanne-Allen-2/publica tion/305060806_The_theory-practice_gap_Turning_theory_into_practice_in_a_pre-ser vice_teacher_education_program/links/591ba63d4585153b614fa8c8/The-theory-practi ce-gap-Turning-theory-into-practice-in-a-pre-service-teacher-education-program.pdf

Doe, T. (2011). *Teacher professional learning partnerships in practice.* CQUniversity. http://pstorage-cqu-2209908187.s3.amazonaws.com/25848056/cqu_8123SOUR CE2SOURCE2.5.pdf

Hattie, J. (2009). *Visible learning: A synthesis of over 800 meta-analyses relating to achievement.* Routledge. www.taylorfrancis.com/books/mono/10.4324/9780203887332/visible-learning-john-hattie

Ingvarson, L., Beavis, A., Danielson, C., Ellis, L., & Elliott, A. (2005). *An evaluation of the Bachelor of Learning Management at Central Queensland University.* https://research.acer.edu.au/cgi/viewcontent.cgi?article=1005&context=teacher_education

Lin, Y. (2014). Teacher involvement in school decision making. *Journal of Studies in Education,* 4(3), 50. https://doi.org/10.5296/jse.v4i3.6179

Lynch, D. (2012). *Preparing teachers in times of change: Teaching school, standards, new content and evidence.* https://doi.org/10.53333/PRHPG/280209

Marzano, R. J., & Pickering, D. (2006). *Dimensions of learning teacher's manual.* Hawker Browlow.

Smith, R., & Lynch, D. E. (2010). *Rethinking teacher education: Teacher education in a knowledge age.* https://doi.org/10.53333/AACLM/440245

Stecher, B. M., Holtzman, D. J., Garet, M. S., Hamilton, L. S., Engberg, J., Steiner, E. D., Robyn, A., Baird, M. D., Gutierrez, I. A., & Peet, E. D. (2018). *Improving teaching effectiveness. Final report: The intensive partnerships for effective teaching through 2015–2016.* https://findresults.issuelab.org/resources/30998/30998.pdf

Wenner, J. A., & Campbell, T. (2016). The theoretical and empirical basis of teacher leadership: A review of the literature. *Review of Educational Research,* 87(1), 134–171. https://doi.org/10.3102/0034654316653478

14 The teaching transformation agenda

In this chapter, we resolve the conundrum around the teaching transformation agenda by identifying seven "agenda items" that now represent immediate steps for changing education, schooling, and teacher education in line with what this book has suggested. There have been enough government reports and ongoing debates about education, schooling, and teacher education to realise that the time has come for the profession to change course. Reviewing our commentary in the preceding 13 chapters, it becomes apparent that transforming what is now a 200-year-old system strongly influenced by the logic of the industrial age is challenging. At its heart, change propositions fundamentally react to a sustained cultural problem because of the power of the status quo, the lack of clarity about the purpose of schooling, and a lack of coherent understanding of the field of education and its complexity. Further complicating it all is the emergence of digital media platforms that have enabled innumerable voices to enter debates about transforming education, hijacking or clouding pertinent issues. In addition, the reward systems do not appear robust enough for anyone, from politicians to education system leaders to school staff and university academics, to consider transformative, sustainable change as we have outlined. Such discussions seem only to happen on the fringes of mainstream education.

This is all compounded when one considers that we are living in times of ongoing exponential technological innovation and disruption. Trying to pin something down is difficult, not unlike holding back the tide. A significant problem is that the profession, particularly classroom teachers and their school leaders, are becoming exhausted just trying to keep the current system operating, let alone radically changing it. The international problem of teacher shortages should be seen as the proverbial canary in the coal mine. This might be a comment about society's political leaders not having the gumption to resolve what it means to be educated. It is a challenging undertaking that probably does not offer any political advantage given the short horizons due to the election cycle and lack of meaningful discussion in the daily news cycle. Adding more things to the curriculum to appease a lobby group or deal with an emergent social issue, keeping the school day the same because that is the expected norm, and reinforcing old teaching mindsets and logic are not the solutions. Nor are simple remedies like embracing the latest educational fad, conducting yet another review into teacher education,

DOI: 10.4324/9781003303312-18

or throwing more money at the same old problem. There must be a new agenda, and the profession needs to take agency over it.

Before concluding with our seven teaching transformation agenda items, we first recap what we have covered in the book as a frame for these items. In Chapter 1, we explained how exponential technological and societal changes profoundly impact people's lives and how work is undertaken. At the centre of the discussion was a call for change in a system of schooling that has hallmarks from an era now long past. Because schools prepare young people for the future, and society has changed fundamentally and will continue to do so, schools must change accordingly. In Chapter 2, we explored these societal changes further by examining the concept of a Knowledge Society. This revealed a set of impacts on schools that we argued have a direct implication for those who teach. To exemplify the effects of a Knowledge Society, in Chapter 3, we explored the government's actions in Australia, England, and the United States to reveal an education landscape that tells a repeating story of what can only be described as education in crisis. Chapter 4 focused on the question of "What does it mean to be educated?" We suggested in this chapter that a national narrative is needed to underpin answering such a question, and we firmly implicated government leadership in undertaking such a task. We responded to the framing of this question in Chapter 5 by identifying three lenses for rethinking the curriculum in a school: (i) wellbeing as the centrepiece of curriculum aspirations, (ii) dealing with old and new knowledge, and (iii) education and its interplay within and for society.

In Chapter 6, we investigated the notion of "teaching transformation" as a backdrop for a set of change propositions we made in the subsequent chapters. We explained the concept of "teaching transformation" and contrasted it with "teaching improvement" agendas to point out that teaching transformation is a radical rethink of teaching. It means an end to ongoing "tinkering". Again, we reinforced the idea that using all that is known about teaching effectiveness, social change, technological innovation and disruption, not to mention explosions in understanding the neuroscience of the brain, the emergence of artificial intelligence, and engaging in client-centric models, was needed as reference points to create new approaches to teaching which are fit for the future. Chapter 7 began a sign-off from the education past by presenting a different approach to how teaching is organised in our schools and creating an agenda for a revolution in the role and function of what is universally known as the schoolteacher. Key to our logic is the creation of (teaching) "consultants" who lead teaching transformation in schools by engineering workforce stratification and engaging multi-disciplinary teams in the schooling equation. Ultimately, we suggest expanding their role, not unlike how the medical profession has achieved specialist roles that have advanced patient care, into specialist educational functions centred on complex learning design, diagnostic and education process advice, and guidance to those "involved others" in schools. Accordingly, the consultant would coordinate these multi-disciplinary professionals in actioning and achieving outcomes specified in individual learning plans.

Chapter 8 expanded the premise of this new school teaching logic to identify six fundamental and interrelated concepts: (i) education as a specialist field, (ii) codified teaching practice, (iii) scope of practice, (iv) workplace stratification, (v) teachers as researchers, and (vi) increased teacher agency. An interplay of these concepts, as mooted in previous chapters, can be understood as a "new grammar of schooling". In Chapter 9, a new grammar of schooling was explained as movements away from age-related student groupings, the division of learning into subjects, and "one-size fits all approaches" that are synonymous with what young people currently experience. A new grammar of schooling would see schools move towards client-centric models. We used six key considerations to locate and explain the new grammar of schooling. We envision (i) the school as a nursery for future citizens and (ii) engineering schools as centres of care and wellbeing, (iii) systems to support and enable a new approach to teaching, (iv) a new model for school leadership and management, (v) the exploitation of technology for teaching and learning effects, and (vi) the exploration of a new education market to stimulate innovation and disruption for futures-oriented teaching and learning impacts. Chapter 10 continued the themes from Chapter 9 by investigating (i) technology-rich environments, (ii) new systems of education, and (iii) the education market. Chapters 11 and 12 focused the book on preparing a different type of teacher. These chapters effectively provided a blueprint for how teaching transformation work can be actioned. We outlined our thinking on preparing a new teaching construct by identifying seven concepts that together scope the goals of a teacher preparation program. These are (i) stratification of teaching work, (ii) a scope of practice, (iii) education as a specialist field, (iv) teachers as researchers, (v) teacher agency, (vi) codified teaching, and (vii) a mechanism to address the theory–practice divide. The theory–practice conundrum, which is an issue in teacher education at present, we explored in Chapter 12 by identifying five innovative mechanisms: (i) new teacher education pathways, (ii) teaching schools as the place for learning to teach and for furthering the evidence base of the profession, (iii) portal tasks as the focus for what needs to be learnt and demonstrated for graduation, (iv) new content required to be learnt, and (v) a model for learning how to teach. In Chapter 13, we sought to understand what has been done before in the teaching transformation space, take stock of the critical elements that need to be considered for success, and to consider how these inform our teaching transformation ideas. We sought to learn about undertaking transformation in education, teaching, and schooling, ensuring our proposals have a high chance of success by reviewing the associated research evidence and issues experienced in the past that hindered innovations from taking hold. A key and interesting finding is that educational research is not packaged ready for teacher consumption and that there are very few large-scale and longitudinal studies into teacher education, especially from the perspective of graduate teachers' capabilities – how well they can teach and their life cycles post-graduation.

Having reviewed what we have covered in this book, we conclude the book with seven agenda items. These represent the critical work that now needs to be undertaken if a "teaching transformation" is to occur. We start by picking up a key theme from Chapter 4, the role of governments in the teaching transformation agenda.

Teaching transformation agenda #1: Governments must show leadership in defining the society they want to engineer

The first important consideration in any transformational agenda is leadership. It requires top-level buy-in, which implies a level of courage. Change requires clarity of purpose followed by robust, committed, and informed leadership for success. In authoring this book, we have endeavoured to generate the required insight for "key agents" to now take carriage of the transformation of teaching, schooling, and teacher education. However, this needs to be triggered by leadership at the political level. This agenda item is about governments creating an instructive national narrative that defines the society "we" want young people to grow up in and contribute to and accordingly constitute a coherent curriculum for our schools. This underpins a curriculum standpoint that appreciates that knowledge and one's capacity to exploit it in new and interconnected ways is crucial to success in our modern world. This points to a series of 21st-century skills needing to be honed by students and, accordingly, in contexts far removed from the past's pencil-and-paper classroom regimes. This alone does not scope the complete "new curriculum" because, as our commentaries have indicated, exponential change has a fundamental impact on humans; accordingly, preparing people to live with and embrace uncertainty is the new civics curriculum. This needs governments to define "what is in" and "what is out" and, in doing so, declutter the curriculum and allow schools and teachers clarity on what being educated means and to fill in the gaps for students as individuals. We lament the rise of the populist politician in all this and decry the banalities of modern political-centric debates about education. We call for a return of the visionary "statesperson" who builds on life experiences, listens to the research evidence, and articulates its benefits in a way that engages the population! Perhaps this book can start a revolution along these lines.

Teaching transformation agenda #2: New success criteria

As we have argued in early chapters, long-established norms and ways of doing things in society are in flux. A personal capacity to not only operate within such circumstances – that is, earn a living, raise a family, and pursue one's interest and passions – but also thrive in it are arguably the hallmarks of success in this modern society. We mentioned that success in modern society has another important dimension: coming to terms with one's humanity in a world where personal well-being gets lost in the seductive and compelling vortex of screen time and social media. We captured these intents with the idea of creating new success criteria. In effect, this new success criteria logic responds to a refined curriculum, as in the previous agenda item, but it also recognises that "success" in modern society takes many forms. It rounds off discussions about the world we want for our future citizens and thus motivates them to succeed and be acknowledged for that success in new and different ways. Not unlike the Knowledge Society that it all represents. For those in education, it also points to the need for different types of schools and a journey of education that is not defined by just getting into university or achieving a qualification but ongoing learning and adaptation through life.

Teaching transformation agenda #3: A new grammar of schooling is required

The central organisational feature of current schooling is mass education. This is an affront to the life potentials of every young person enrolled, in that no system that makes decisions for the masses will ever be able to ensure every individual succeeds. In a Knowledge Society, a personal capacity to deal with knowledge in unique and creative ways is now a centrepiece of employment. To fall through the gaps in school today is a sure passage to an unfulfilled life. Surely, allowing such an outcome is modern society's greatest social justice issue. Schools must transition to client-centric models, and this transition is dependent upon a teaching workforce positioned to deal with students as individuals and a teaching repertoire focused on codified evidence-based approaches to guarantee optimal outcomes. A new grammar of schooling means we need a fundamental and strategic reset of the "what, when, where and how" young people are taught the "new curriculum". This new grammar is built on a simple yet powerful logic that emphasises the importance of teacher agency in the student's learning process. It rethinks schooling of old around a clear focus on teachers applying specific education knowledge for individual student learning outcome effects. However, it also pre-supposes new ways of organising teacher work beyond the classroom. The teacher has to be all things to all students, and teaching happens within the four walls of a classroom. This invokes technology, but it also imagines new education markets, new operating logics for what is a school, and "qualification regimes" that represent new life cycles of work and home life. It also means teachers have to learn new things in new ways!

Teaching transformation agenda #4: Teacher preparation attuned to a specialist body of education knowledge and teaching skills, honed in and for real work contexts

The propositions that a new grammar of schooling and a rethought teacher construct represent are all commensurate to specialist teaching knowledge and codified practice. This implicates both the teacher preparation regime and the organisational logic of future schools. We believe teacher education is the place to start. Teacher education has undergone numerous reviews across the globe, citing the inadequacies of current organisational regimes. Our book has identified five mechanisms for reforming teacher education: (i) new teacher education pathways, (ii) teaching schools as the place for learning to teach and for furthering the evidence base of the profession, (iii) portal tasks as the focus for what needs to be learnt and demonstrated for graduation, (iv) new content required to be learnt, and (v) a new model for learning how to teach. Taken together, these mechanisms blueprint a rethink on teacher education and can potentially seed the growth of a highly skilled and Knowledge Society-centric teacher. The BLM experience detailed in Chapter 13 does not augur well for teaching transformation agendas. However, with clarity of purpose, committed leadership, and consideration of the points we've made throughout this book, including considering the obstacles apparent in the BLM experience, we believe there is a viable way forward in the teacher education space.

We acknowledge that teacher education is somewhat a "chicken and egg" for teaching transformation. It requires competency with the new agenda in both schools and teacher education faculties, as well as in teachers who are experts and committed to that agenda. To this end, we signal that teacher education pro-gramming at all levels of the profession must go beyond the ad hoc release from class models that predominate the classroom teacher's life. It must find ways to address the theory–practice divide resulting from the most common on-campus and practicum model of initial teacher education and move to a new set of strati-fied teacher education qualifications. A stratification of the teaching workforce creates a new schooling capacity for teaching the curriculum to all learners and acknowledges specialist expertise. Teaching transformation requires a transforma-tion in how the school and teacher education business is organised. Third-space thinking – which is the organising principles informing the "teaching school" concept – is all about each party (i.e. the school, the university, and others) being acknowledged as having an equal yet different contribution to make (i.e. in the co-design of programs), and that improvement work is done in partnership for global teaching and teacher education improvement effects.

Teaching transformation agenda #5: Introducing the "consultant" role as a catalyst for change

In Chapter 7, we introduced the (teaching) "consultant" concept. These con-sultants have a transition role in the birth of a new grammar of schooling and in teacher education changes. However, they are also a strategic mechanism that helps define how learning design works for students in a new grammar of school-ing. As a transitionary role, they embody, at the expert level, the specialist educa-tion knowledge that a new grammar of schooling entails. This specialist-level expertise and leadership positioning build the required teaching capabilities as the key role in a stratified teaching work environment. In an operational sense, the role of consultants, which we have co-opted from the logic of how the medical profession organises its specialists in hospitals, provides complex learning design, diagnostic and education process advice, and guidance to those "involved others" and accordingly coordinates these multi-disciplinary professionals into actioning and achieving outcomes specified in individual learning plans. Consultants repre-sent the career pinnacle for teachers and are achieved not through time served but higher levels of specific role-oriented formal education and the regular upgrading of their stock of complex knowledge, and ultimately by achieving membership of "the" pedagogical professional association. Once again, we reference how medical specialists hold fellowships in specialist colleges. As a mechanism for change, the preparation and positioning of consultants into schools to effect a new grammar of schooling is also an issue of scale, given that thousands of schools in our various education systems need to be transformed. However, we contend this is a strategy for creating higher levels of teacher agency in education. The knock-on effect here is that the role of the school head changes from managing a system of mass education to one enabling a client-centric system where consultants are representative of teacher agency in education. To trigger this agenda item requires deciding the "new curriculum", configuring a new grammar of schooling, and then identifying candidates for intensive high-level training for "consultant" work. To counter the "chicken-and-egg" situation outlined earlier, we invoke agenda item #1 – government actions – and then changes to teacher education along the lines outlined in Chapters 11 and 12.

Teaching transformation agenda #6: A stratified set of teaching roles

Stratification is about sustainably repositioning teachers for complex and multi-dimensional work. It can be understood as a new set of teaching roles within a new grammar of schooling, and for each new teacher role, it is a defining scope of practice. Scope of practice means teachers are no longer individuals positioned to be all things to all students. Teaching workloads are client-centric, commensurate to role scope and multi-disciplinary team capacities. We propose three levels of teachers: teaching associates, registered (or certified) teachers, and consultants. The key point is that this stratification refreshes the current school/classroom-centric model by clarifying roles, capitalising on specialist functions for designed effects, and creating a sense of agency for incumbents and their assigned tasks. It also creates a foundation for multi-disciplinary teams to enter the school as productive and organised professionals to optimise student learning and wellbeing outcomes. On a related plane, our consultant role acts as a transitionary strategy in early stratification iterations but lays the foundations for new practice models as the teaching profession matures. This will further manifest with new the educational markets that enhanced teacher agency generates.

In many ways, the solution for transformed teaching resides in teachers having the required agency in their own business, which, one could argue, is very low in Australia, the United States, and England. Teacher agency means teachers have a more significant influence and control of their profession and, accordingly, would see its esteem rising in the public's minds. It is a "chicken-and-egg" thing again. Teacher agency is commensurate to high levels of professional teaching prowess, which is commensurate to high levels of teacher education, which requires teachers with high levels of teaching prowess to design and deliver teacher education. Add to the complexity of over-busy and frazzled teachers and teacher educators focused on reward systems contrary to what is required, and it becomes, so it seems, an intractable problem to address. The task becomes doable by starting with a redefined and focused school curriculum, committed top-level leadership, and a preparation regime commensurate to the tasks ahead.

Teaching transformation agenda #7: Increasing research into education, teaching, and teacher education and packaging it for teacher consumption

At the heart of such calls for change in schooling, teaching, and teacher education is a deficient body of research evidence to inform and guide the preparation and practice of teachers. This problem is compounded by educational research not being packaged or organised to be instructive to the work of teachers. The available research is often small scale, incomplete, narrowly focused, and published behind paywalls in formats that inform other researchers but are not instructive for teachers, their work, and their professional growth and development. This means governments must match their numerous reviews with strategically funded research agendas that focus on answering questions that matter for the curriculum agendas they confirm, ultimately preparing and positioning the teaching profession for required work. As we outlined early in this book, people who work in education know that there are many moving parts to contend with when changes are mooted in the constructs of schooling, teaching, and teacher education. These three constructs, individually and especially when considered together, form a complex system with many knock-on effects when an element in the prevailing system of things is altered. These effects are often unanticipated and surprising and may cause problems elsewhere in the system. For individual actors in this system, enacting change can end careers when plans contradict dominant cultural norms and positions. This should not be a disincentive to trying. What is needed is a logical, defensible, and engaging "why" to promote increased levels of psychological safety within schools and systems – the reason for this book. This will enable courageous actors to move toward change, with the security of research evidence paving the way and mitigating catastrophic failure.

In concluding this book, we acknowledge again that schooling as we know it in Western countries is steeped in tradition, with long-standing practices and norms valued because they have been in place for decades or even centuries. These are the sacred cows that may need to be sacrificed. Schools are very busy workplaces, and the constant seems to be change, role creep, and an increasingly crowded curriculum. While teachers are over-busy, teacher educators' reward system focuses on publishing in their chosen fields rather than effecting change. This lack of alignment further complicates and dilutes any willingness to do more than publish about change and certainly not to guide reform. In crafting our seven agenda items, we have attempted to focus on what we think represents a set of potent levers for change. While the levers themselves are potent, they still need brave people to pull them.

As the previous chapters have shown, we recognise the difficulties of generating and sustaining change in the education field. Moreover, as former classroom schoolteachers, we recognise that frontline teachers prioritise the interests of children and are interested in anything that can assist them in their complex everyday work. Our experience since the 1960s reinforces the position that blockages to change, reform, and transformation in education can arise beyond the classroom in the ideological fields of what Australian First Nations leader Noel Pearson refers to as the "ideology-producers" in universities and bureaucracies. If teachers resist change, it is primarily because of the ideology reproduction in schools of education and halls of power and regulation – the power of the *status quo*. The material interests, personal investments, and status in these areas have greater priority than what works well for children's learning of curriculum knowledge in schools. They oppose whatever does not fit their ideological slogans or interests, irrespective of what credible research findings might suggest and their lack of data. The trigger for enabling the kinds of transformations we suggest in this book lies with the political class: their lesson is that progressive thinking around teacher preparation and teaching practice, rather than being a democratising influence, often obstructs the visionary outcomes of so much education policy.

Index

Page numbers in **bold** refer to tables.

university and teaching school 118–119
US: education systems in crisis 27–30

"weak signals" 47
wellbeing: care and 47, 92–93; as centrepiece 46; and mastery 47–48; old and

new knowledge 48–49; young and their
37–40
Wilson, S. 59
workplace stratification *see* stratified
teaching workforce